A WALKI

HONG

Sketches of the city's architectural treasures...

Take a stroll through Hong Kong old and new

plus Explore the wonders of Macau

SECOND EDITION

Gregory Byrne Bracken

All text and illustrations by Gregory Byrne Bracken

Published by Marshall Cavendish Editions
An imprint of Marshall Cavendish International
1 New Industrial Road
Singapore 536196
genrefsales@sg.marshallcavendish.com
www.marshallcavendish.com/genref

Marshall Cavendish is a trademark of Times Publishing Limited

Other Marshall Cavendish offices:
Marshall Cavendish Corporation, 99 White Plains Road, Tarrytown NY 10591-9001, USA • Marshall Cavendish International (Thailand) Co Ltd, 253 Asoke, 12th Floor, Sukhumvit 21 Road, Klongtoey Nua, Wattana, Bangkok 10110, Thailand • Marshall Cavendish (Malaysia) Sdn Bhd, Times Subang, Lot 46, Subang Hi-Tech Industrial Park, Batu Tiga, 40000 Shah Alam, Selangor Darul Ehsan, Malaysia

First edition published in 2003 by Times Media Pte Ltd

A CIP record for this book is available from the British Library

ISBN 978-981-4361-41-5

Printed and bound in Singapore by KWF Printing Pte Ltd

For my mother, Maura, who always loved Kowloon

"So you live for today and to hell with everything, grab what you can, because tomorrow, who knows? Don't get in the way! People are rougher here because everything really is precarious, and nothing lasts in Hong Kong."

— James Clavell, *Noble House*

Contents

Acknowledgments

I would like to thank Melvin Neo, Chris Newson, Justin Lau and Benson Tan at Marshall Cavendish for their wonderful support on this project.

Introduction

History

When Hong Kong became a British colony in 1841, it consisted only of the island itself and the district of Kowloon on the Chinese mainland to the north. A larger area of the mainland — the New Territories — was leased only in 1898. Hong Kong rapidly became a centre for the opium industry, and soon established itself as a vital trading post and gateway to China.

Entrepreneurs have always flourished in Hong Kong, more than almost anywhere else on earth, thanks in part to the Chinese work ethic and the relatively laissez-faire administration of the British. Hong Kong's economy grew steadily — though mostly still overshadowed as an international trading centre by its neighbour, Shanghai. Then on 8 December 1941, Japan attacked, and on Christmas Day, Hong Kong fell. Under the Japanese, the population plummeted from 1.6 million to 0.6 million. It seemed that the third port of the British Empire was of little use to them and they let it fall into destitution. After the Allied victory in August 1945, U.S. President Franklin Roosevelt wanted the British to hand the colony back to China. British Prime Minister Winston Churchill did not agree.

What eventually turned Hong Kong into the economic powerhouse it is today was the Communist takeover of China in 1949. Suddenly Hong Kong was flooded with Chinese refugees, some of them rich, knowledgeable industrialists and others, the huge labour force needed to spearhead the economy. Many of these refugees were from Shanghai. Hong Kong, with its magnificent harbour, stable and honest government and low tax rates, proved perfect for enterprise. As a result, industrial growth was rapid. The population soon grew from 2.4 million in 1955 to 5.6 million in 1988.

On July 1997, Hong Kong was returned to China and became a Special Administrative Region (SAR). Under the "one country, two systems" formula, it was exempted from the mainland's socialist system, and continues to have a relatively high degree of autonomy in its political, legal and economic affairs — guaranteed until 2047.

Did You Know?
Hong Kong occupies an area of only around 1100 sq km but has a population of about seven million.

Climate

Hong Kong has a sub-tropical humid climate. January and February are the coolest months although the weather can be variable. In March and April the temperature and humidity begin to rise — mist and low clouds can obscure the Peak for days. The months from May through September are hot and humid. From late July to mid-October, there is an increased risk of typhoons — violent tropical storms that can cause structural damage and loss of life. The best months to visit are October through December, when humidity drops and sunny days are followed by cool nights.

Dress

You should dress lightly and comfortably, but remember that you will not be allowed into places like mosques and temples wearing shorts or short-sleeved shirts. Shoes should be removed before entering certain buildings, especially mosques, but sometimes houses and offices will expect you to do so as well.

Did You Know?
The word "typhoon" comes from the Cantonese *tai fung*, which means "great wind".

Spelling

Spelling can sometimes differ in and around Hong Kong and Macau, whether on maps, in guides or even on street signs. The names and spellings in this guidebook have been standardised for consistency.

Key to Icons

 Must See

 Drinking

 National Monument

 Eating

 Good View

 Shopping

 See At Night

Suggested Itineraries

History
Sheung Wan
Wan Chai
Kowloon South
Further Afield
Macau

Culture
Wan Chai
Kowloon South

Shopping
Central
Wan Chai
Causeway Bay
Kowloon South

Markets
Wan Chai
Kowloon North

Colonial City
Central
Kowloon South
Macau

For Children
Kowloon South
Further Afield

East Asia

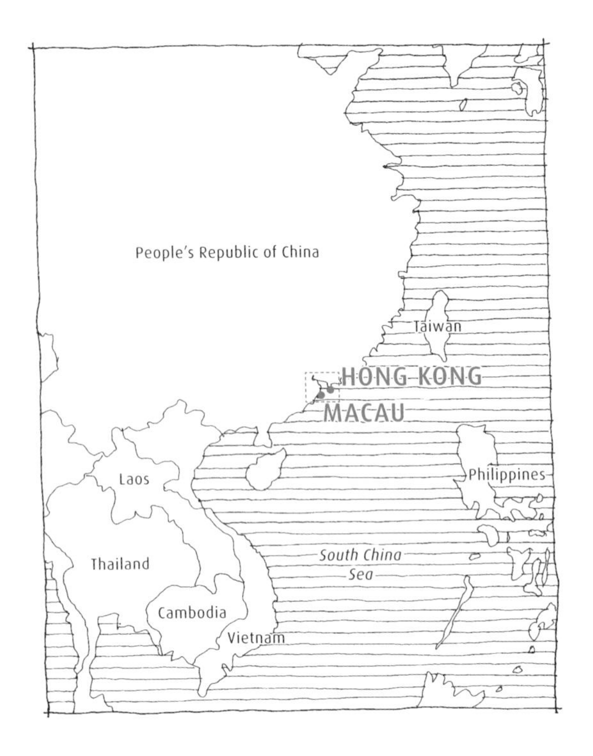

People's Republic of China
Taiwan
HONG KONG
MACAU
Philippines
Laos
Thailand
South China
Sea
Cambodia
Vietnam

Hong Kong & Macau

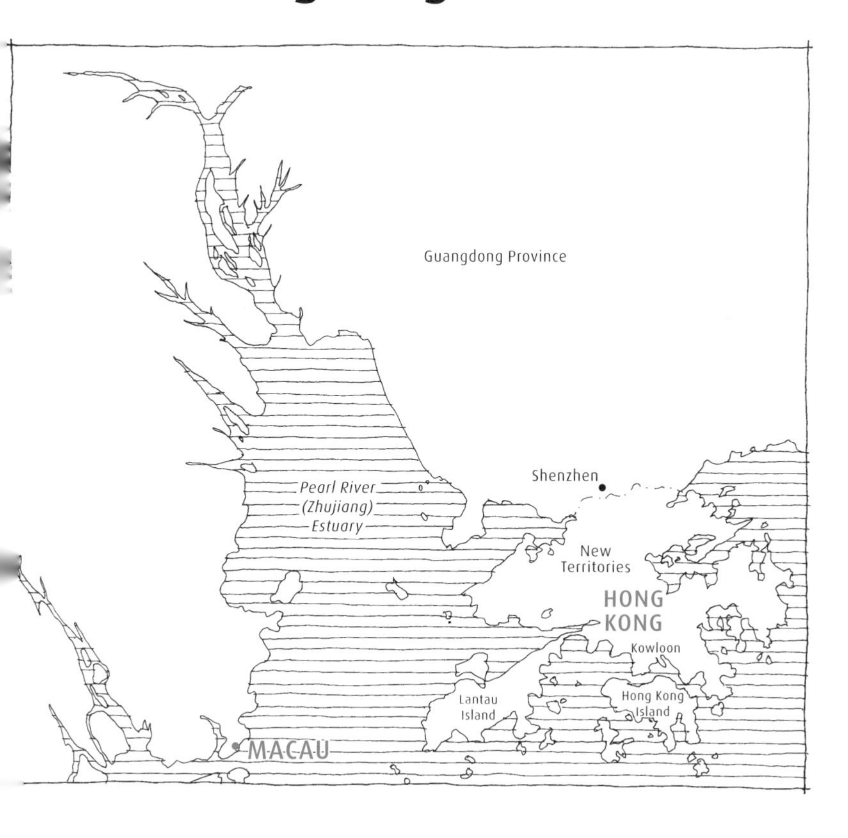

Hong Kong Island & Kowloon

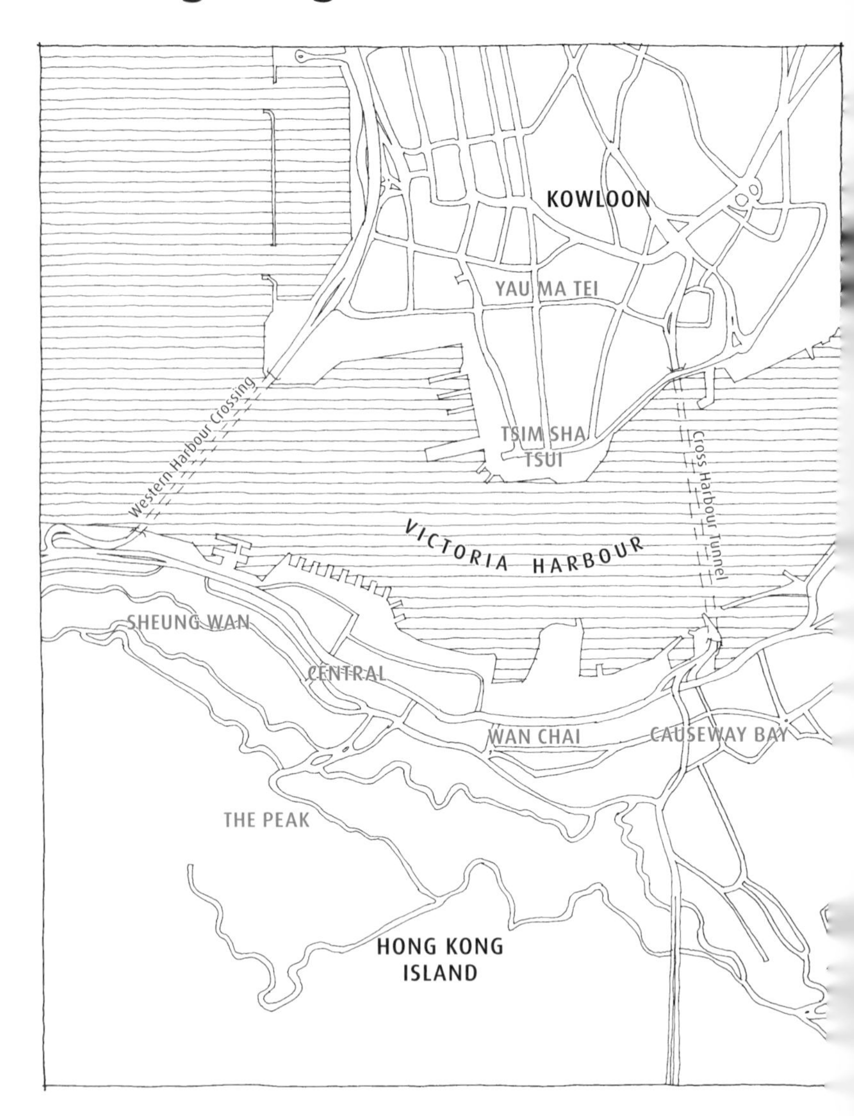

Note: There is no bridge across Victoria Harbour; to move between Hong Kong Island and Kowloon, take either the underground rail (MTR), the road tunnels, or — best of all — the legendary Star Ferry.

Sheung Wan

Nearest Tram Stop: Des Voeux Road West at Western Street
Approximate walking time: 1 hour 30 minutes

Sheung Wan

This area just west of Central is one of the oldest and most authentically Chinese parts of the city. Despite extensive redevelopment, small pockets of old communities and traditional shops, which have changed little over the generations, can be found throughout the area. This district is also one of the best places in the world to buy Chinese art and antiques, especially the streets around Hollywood Road and Cat Street.

SHEUNG WAN

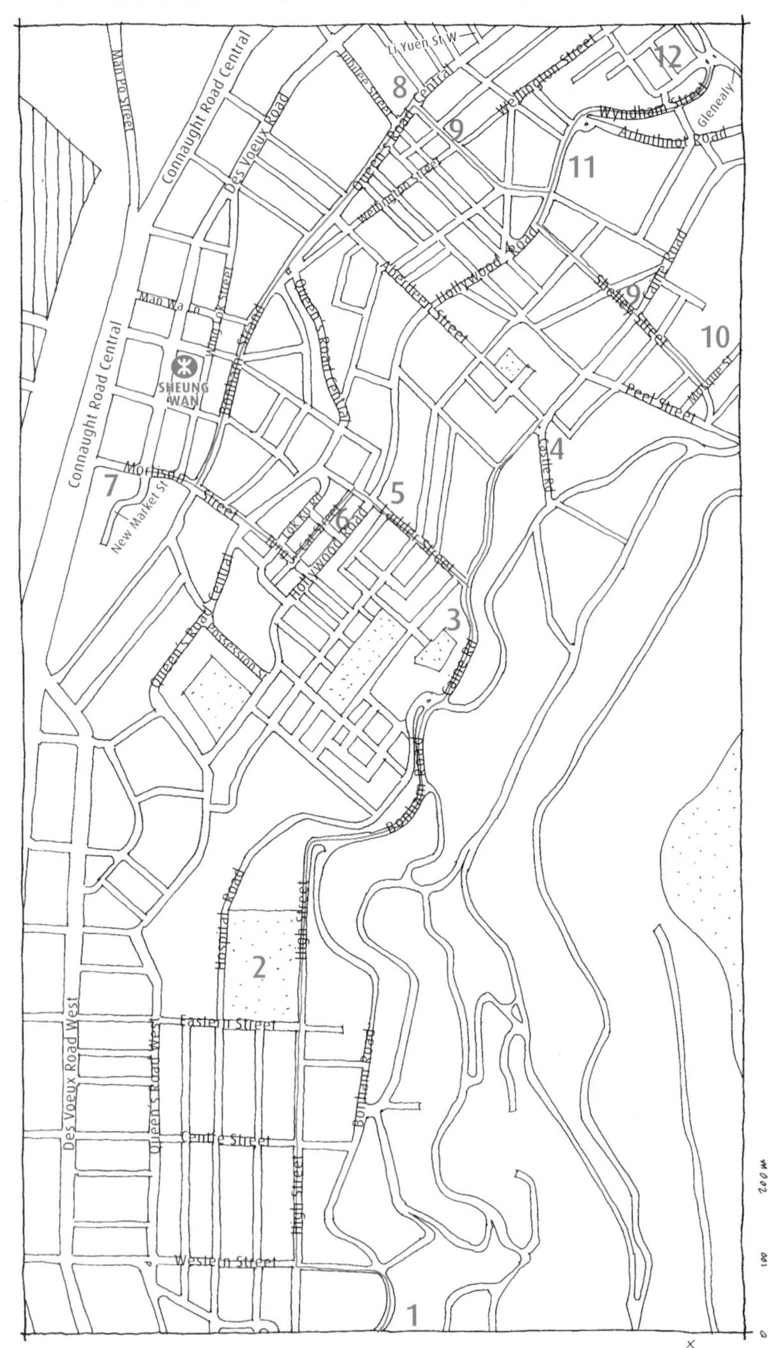

Li Yuen St W
Jubilee Street
Man Po Street
Connaught Road Central
Des Voeux Road
Queen's Road Central
Wellington Street
Wyndham Street
Glenealy
Arbuthnot Road
Hollywood Road
Aberdeen Street
Shelley Street
Caine Road
Peel Street
Mosque St
Castle Rd
Man Wa Ln
Wing Lok Street
SHEUNG WAN
Bonham Strand
Morrison Street
New Market St
Lok Ku Rd
Ladder Street
Possession St
Bonham Road
Hospital Road
High Street
Eastern Street
Des Voeux Road West
Queen's Road West
Centre Street
Western Street
1
2
3
4
5
6
7
8
9
10
11
12
0
100
200m

KEY

1. University of Hong Kong
2. George V Park
3. Museum of Medical Sciences
4. Dr Sun Yat-sen Museum
5. Man Mo Temple
6. Hollywood Road
7. Western Market
8. Central Market
9. Escalator
10. Jamia Mosque
11. Central Police Station Compound
12. Lan Kwai Fong

University of Hong Kong ❶

The campus of the University of Hong Kong boasts some of the best examples of British colonial architecture on the island. The main buildings are Edwardian and Neoclassical in style, and are attractively disposed on the hillside along the western end of Bonham Road. Universities were founded in China from the 1880s onwards and were usually started by Christian missionaries. But in Hong Kong a group of businessmen felt that there should be a secular university following those found in Britain. Governor Sir Frederick Lugard set aside land for the campus, and with donations from local philanthropists, the UK government, the Viceroy of Canton, and overseas Chinese communities, the establishment of the University of Hong Kong quickly gained momentum, and in 1912 it formally opened and took in the first cohort of students.

The campus is also home to the **University Museum and Art Gallery**, housed in the Fung Ping Shan Building at 94 Bonham Road. Hong Kong's oldest museum, it is renowned for its collection of bronzes and ceramics. There are three main periods of bronzes represented by the various items: vessels from the Shang and Zhou Dynasties; mirrors from the Warring States period; and crosses from the Yuan Dynasty. The ceramics collection includes Han Dynasty funerary urns as well as more recent works from other parts of China.

University Museum and Art Gallery
9.30am–6pm Mon–Sat; 1–6pm Sun
Admission free
www.hku.hk/hkumag

George V Park ❷

Leaving the museum, turn right onto Bonham Road, then left onto Western Street. Take the first right onto High Street and follow it until you see George V Park on your left. The park is located in the heart of this old and very Chinese part of the city and was built for the poor. The well-maintained grounds are a pleasure to stroll in and there are sports facilities to be found here as well. Overlooking the park on the High Street side is the **Sai Ying Pun Community Complex**. It is an attractive granite building consisting of a double row of arches that start at street level and then soar up and away from the ground because of the steep slope of High Street.

Sai Ying Pun Community Complex

Museum of Medical Sciences ❸

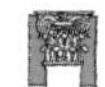

Follow High Street to the end where it merges with Bonham Road, then follow the road until it becomes Caine Road, then take the first left onto **Ladder Street** — a long, wide staircase typical of many of the streets in this hilly part of town.

Take the first left down another staircase-laneway and you will see the **Museum of Medical Sciences** on your left at No. 2 Caine Lane. This handsome Edwardian building was built in 1906 as the Bacteriological Institute, founded to combat the

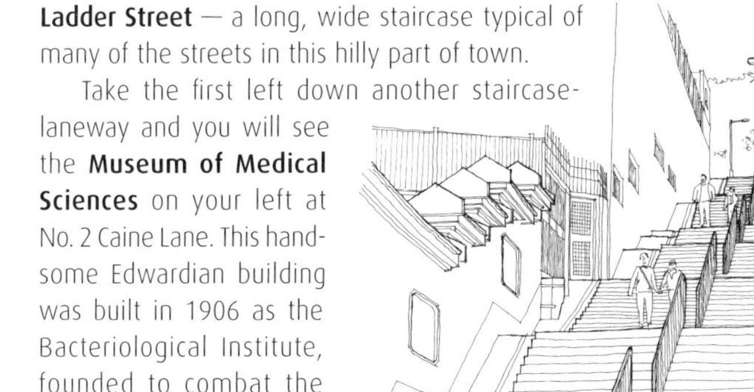

Ladder Street

plague epidemics that gripped Hong Kong beginning in 1894. British patients were treated upstairs, Chinese patients in the basement. The building was restored in 1996 and converted into a museum of Chinese and Western medicine.

Museum of Medical Sciences
10am–5pm Tue–Sat; 1–5pm Sun and public holidays
Admission charges
www.hkmms.org.hk

Did You Know?
It was in Hong Kong that the Japanese scientist, Dr Shibasaburo Kitasato, first isolated the agent of the bubonic plague. His Swiss colleague, Alexandre Yersin, provided the first accurate description of the plague's bacillus.

Dr Sun Yat-sen Museum ❹

Retrace your step to Caine Road and turn left, and you will come to the Dr Sun Yat-sen Museum perched high over the road on your right. Its entrance is around the corner, at No. 7 Castle Road. This imposing Edwardian mansion was built in 1914 and is now a museum dedicated to the first president of the Republic of China. It concentrates on Dr Sun's time spent as a medical student in Hong Kong. It is also near the route of the Dr Sun Yat-sen Historical Trail, which takes in 15 sites of significance to the man known as the Father of Modern China.

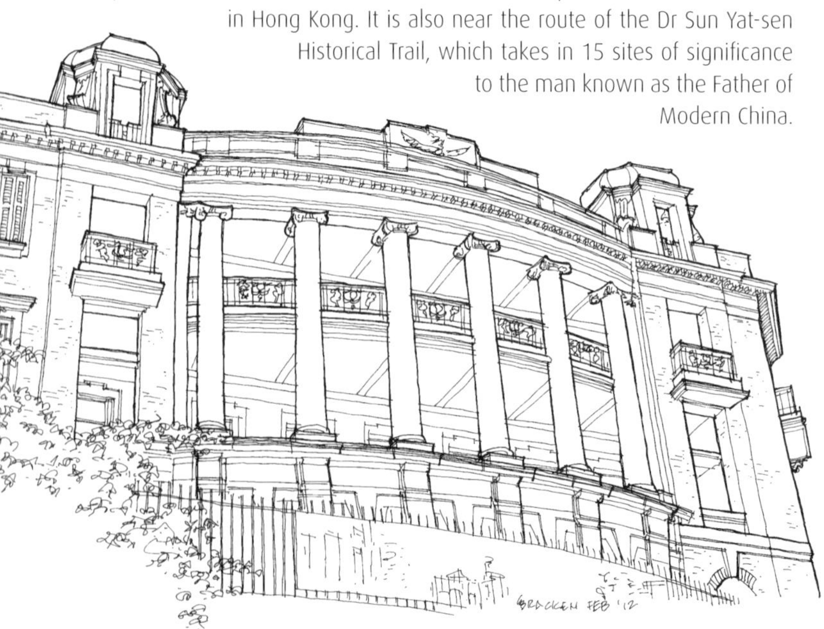

Dr Sun Yat-sen Museum

Aberdeen Street

Facing the museum is **Aberdeen Street**, another of Sheung Wan's steeply sloping stepped streets. Its lower reaches are lined with market stalls.

Dr Sun Yat-sen Museum
10am–6pm Mon–Wed and Fri–Sat; 10am–7pm Sun and public holidays
Admission charges, but free on Wed
www.hk.drsunyatsen.museum
Tel: 2367 6373

Man Mo Temple ❺

Retrace your steps back along Caine Road until you come to Ladder Street again and walk down it until you come to the junction with Hollywood Road. Man Mo Temple will be on your right. Known as the Civil and Military Temple in English, this is one of the oldest and most famous Chinese temples in Hong Kong. Dedicated to two deities — Man, the God of Literature, and Mo, the God of War (who is worshipped by the police as well as the triads) — the exact date of the temple's construction is not known. It is said to have already been standing when the British claimed the island in 1841. The notorious pirate Cheung Po-tsai is also said to have had a hand in its construction, presumably as penance for his evil ways. It was renovated in the mid-19th century. Huge incense coils hanging from the ceiling fill the temple's interior with a fragrant, smoky haze. Outside the entrance are gilt plaques describing the gods being worshipped and a special reminder to all visitors to be quiet.

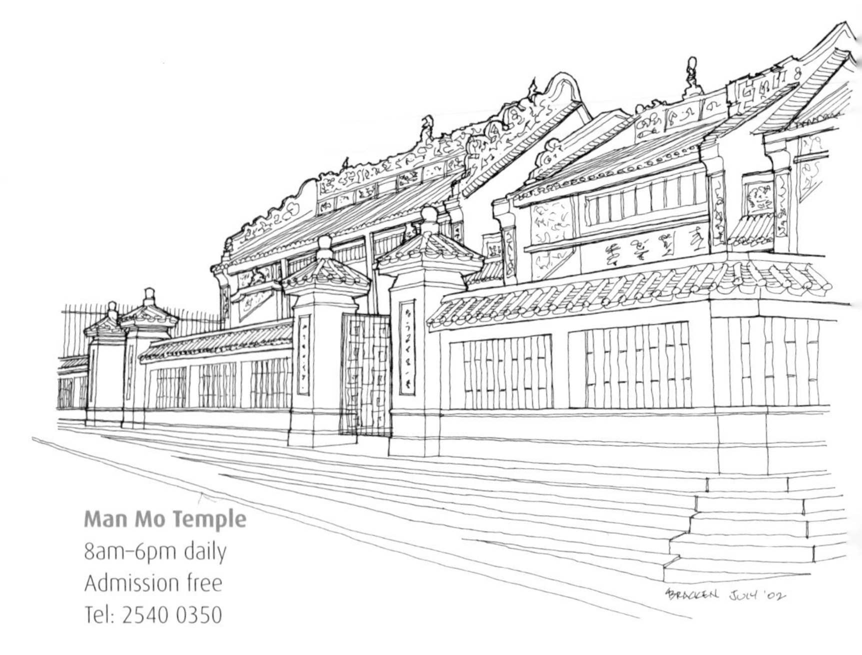

Man Mo Temple
8am–6pm daily
Admission free
Tel: 2540 0350

Hollywood Road ❻

The area around Hollywood Road, Wyndham Street, Wellington Street and Cat Street has to be one of the best places in the world to buy Chinese antiques and curios. It is also one of the most interesting areas in the city just for browsing — the garish signs and colourful banners hung over shopfronts, potted plants balanced precariously on balconies and zig-zagging lines of laundry are unmistakable landmarks. Coupled with the noise from people bargaining at stalls, shouting from doorways, food being fried, the hiss and crackle of televisions and radios and, of course, the traffic, this is a truly unique walking experience.

Cat Street (actual name Lascar Row) is a pedestrian laneway lined with antique and curio shops as well as stalls selling cheap jewellery, ornaments and traditional carvings. It is an ideal place for buying souvenirs. Nearby Man Wa Lane is home to a number of "chop" (Chinese name seal) carvers; they can also do Latin script, and a job takes anything from one to four hours.

Did You Know?
Hollywood Road has nothing to do with American movies. It was named after Governor John Davis's family home in Westbury-on-Trym, near Bristol.

Western Market ❼

At the end of Cat Street, turn right onto Tung Street. Cross Queen's Road Central, and follow Morrison Street until you see the Western Market across Des Voeux Road. This handsome four-storey Edwardian building, built in 1906, used to be one of Hong Kong's principal food markets. In 1991 it was reopened as an arts and crafts shopping centre specialising in traditional Chinese trades, particularly textiles. There are also shops selling antiques and other collectibles, as well as a restaurant on the top floor. The firm behind the renovation, Tao Ho Design Architects, successfully preserved much of the external fabric of the building while creating a nostalgic atmosphere inside.

Western Market
10am–7pm daily, restaurants till 11pm
Admission free

Western Market

Central Market ❽

Return along Morrison Street and turn left onto Bonham Strand and you will come to **Queen's Road Central**. This was the first road the British built on the island (1841–43), which they named in honour of Queen Victoria. Still a major thoroughfare, its convoluted routing harks back to the time before land reclamation when it was by the waterfront. It has since been redeveloped — in a somewhat unspectacular modern manner — but is still home to some traditional shophouses with picturesque balconies and covered arcades. A cluster of such shophouses can be found near the junction with Aberdeen Street.

Continue along Queen's Road Central until you can see the Escalator crossing the

Shophouses, Queen's Road Central

road overhead; **Central Market** will be on your left. An unremarkable and in fact rather ugly building from the outside, its cavernous interior is more like a zoo than a market. Everything from chickens and quail to eels and crab, alive or freshly slaughtered, are on display. The Chinese like their purchases fresh and what better way to ensure that than watch dinner being killed before your eyes. This market is definitely not for the faint-hearted. The smell can also be overpowering. But if you feel up to the challenge, then you are in for an exhilarating experience.

Continue along Queen's Road Central and you will come to the small laneways known as **Li Yuen Street West** and **Li Yuen Street East** on your left. These narrow pedestrian alleys are crammed with stalls selling a wide variety of goods including clothing and fabrics.

Central Market
5am–noon daily

Escalator ❾

Retrace your steps along Queen's Road Central until you come back to the Escalator, which links the residential Mid-Levels with the commercial Central district. It is a strikingly simple mode of public transport. More than 200,000 people use it each day, significantly reducing vehicular traffic between these two crowded areas. Free of charge, the Escalator runs down the hill in the morning and uphill for the rest of the day. Consisting of elevated escalators, moving walkways and a series of linking stairways, the route is covered by a curved roof and is open at the sides to let in air and light. The full journey takes approximately 20 minutes.

Escalator
Downhill 6–10am; uphill 10am–midnight
Admission free

Jamia Mosque ⑩

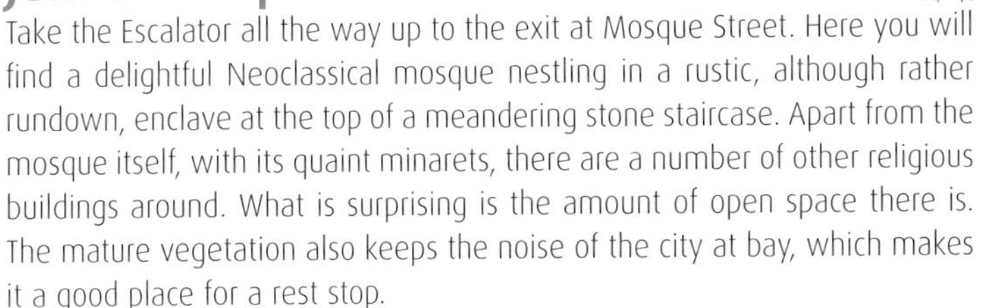

Take the Escalator all the way up to the exit at Mosque Street. Here you will find a delightful Neoclassical mosque nestling in a rustic, although rather rundown, enclave at the top of a meandering stone staircase. Apart from the mosque itself, with its quaint minarets, there are a number of other religious buildings around. What is surprising is the amount of open space there is. The mature vegetation also keeps the noise of the city at bay, which makes it a good place for a rest stop.

Central Police Station Compound ⑪

Walk down towards Hollywood Road and you will see this imposing former police station on your right. The Hong Kong Police Force was formed in 1844, consisting of a small force of 32 men who had been discharged from the military for being unfit to serve. In 1857, Governor Sir Hercules Robinson started reorganising the force, recruiting Indians from the northwest provinces of British India and Chinese from Shandong province in China. The compound, begun in 1841, consists of a number of buildings, including the main police station, a barracks, Victoria Prison, and the former Central Magistracy. It is one of the finest enclaves of colonial architecture left in the city centre, but is unfortunately not open to the public as it awaits redevelopment.

Victoria Prison, located immediately behind the police station, was built in 1841. Heavy corporal punishment began in the 19th century when it was discovered that the Chinese didn't seem to find prison a sufficient deterrent to crime. The Colonial Surgeon then, John Murray, noted that "the Chinese thrive amazingly in confinement and after a few months of incarceration are sent out fat and healthy!" The former **Central Magistracy** is a handsome Edwardian edifice with a heavy stone base, red-brick upper storeys and nicely detailed loggias. It ceased to be a courthouse in 1979 and was declared a monument in 1995.

Lan Kwai Fong ⓬

Follow Hollywood Road as it turns into Wyndham Street, take the first left and you will find yourself in a series of small, sloping pedestrian streets crammed with bars and restaurants, most of which are themed, and nearly all pleasant and interesting. Known as Lan Kwai Fong, during the weekend the various establishments are packed with "chuppies" (Chinese yuppies) and expatriates. This area is also home to a thriving singles scene while the surrounding streets support a number of gay bars.

At No. 2 Lower Albert Road, on the corner of Wyndham Street, is the **Fringe Club**. This Edwardian gem houses one of Hong Kong's most important alternative performance and exhibition spaces. Built originally as a dairy in 1913 (look for the plaque at the top of the facade where it turns the corner), it is a delightful example of the blood-and-bandage style — alternating bands of white plaster and red brick.

Fringe Club
Noon–midnight Mon–Thurs; noon–2am Fri–Sat
Admission free
www.hkfringe.com.hk
Tel: 2521 7485

Fringe Club

Link to The Peak walk: Walk up Glenealy and take the pedestrian underpass until you come to Raimondi College, where you will find the Roman Catholic Cathedral.

The Peak

Nearest MTR Station: Central
Approximate walking time: 1 hour 30 minutes

The Peak

This part of the city was originally home to the Governor's residence as well as Victoria Barracks, part of which has now been transformed into Hong Kong Park. Delightful colonial buildings dot the landscape such as Flagstaff House, now the Teaware Museum, Rawlinson House, a marriage registry, and the Bishop's House, which has been home to the Bishop of St John's Cathedral since the mid-19th century. The Peak, Hong Kong's premier real estate, commands spectacular views of the harbour and can be reached by tram.

THE PEAK

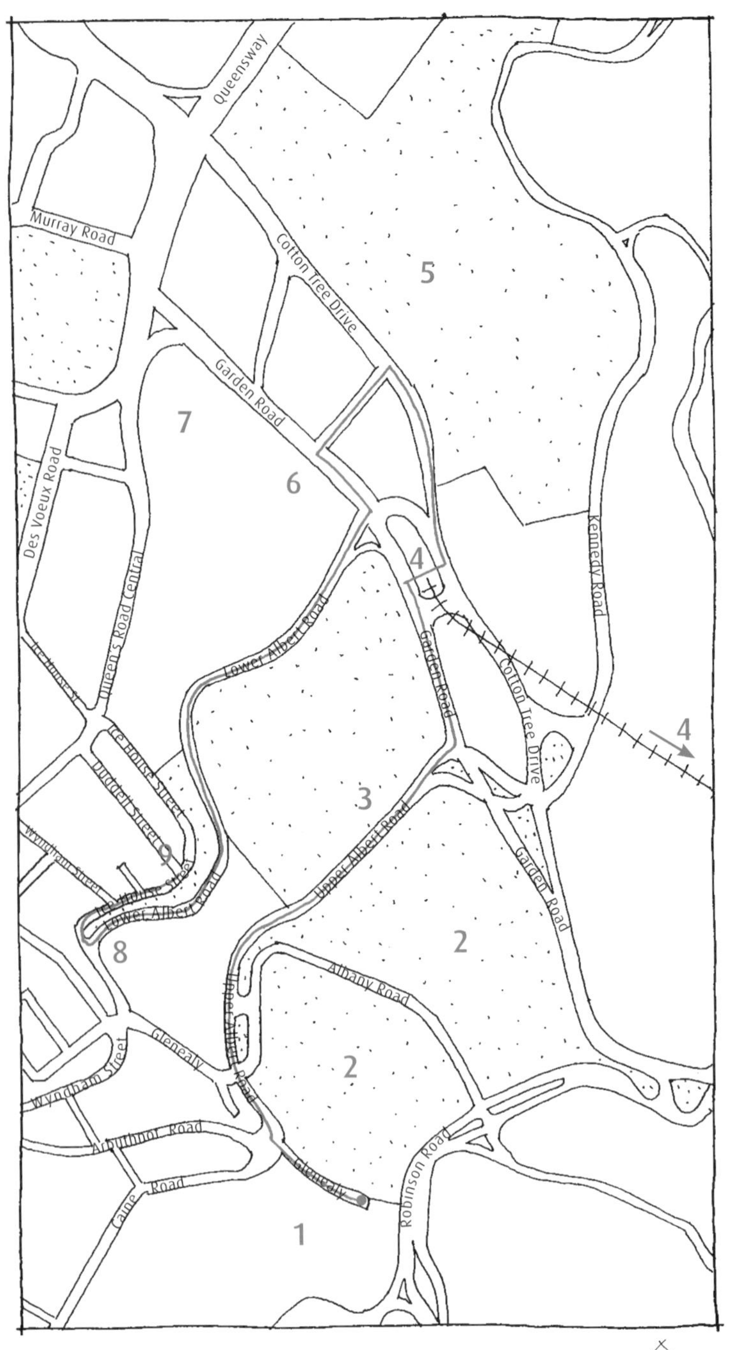
Queensway
Murray Road
Cotton Tree Drive
5
Garden Road
7
6
Des Voeux Road
Queen's Road Central
4
Lower Albert Road
Garden Road
Kennedy Road
Cotton Tree Drive
4
Ice House St
Ice House Street
Duddell Street
3
Upper Albert Road
9
Wyndham Street
Ice House Street
Lower Albert Road
Garden Road
8
2
Albany Road
Upper Albert Road
Glenealy
2
Wyndham Street
Arbuthnot Road
Robinson Road
Glenealy
Caine Road
1
0
100m
200m

KEY

1. Roman Catholic Cathedral
2. Zoological and Botanical Gardens
3. Government House
4. The Peak
5. Hong Kong Park
6. St John's Cathedral
7. French Mission Building (former)
8. Bishop's House
9. Duddell Street

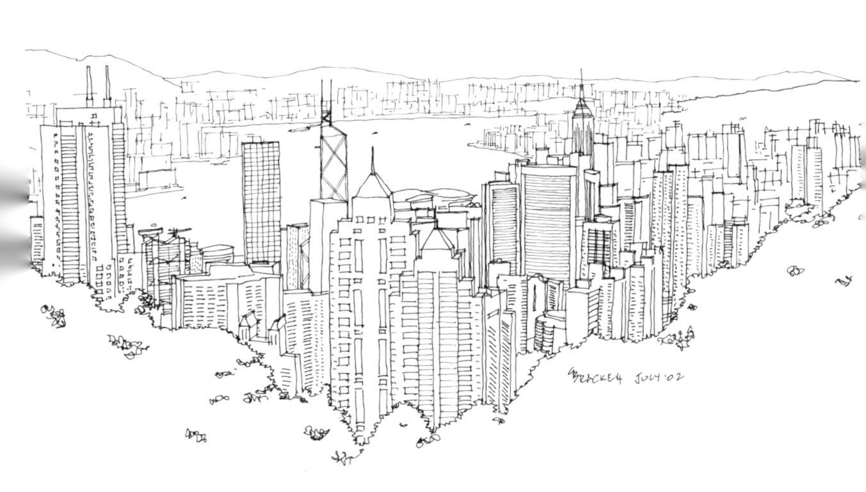

Roman Catholic Cathedral ❶

The Roman Catholic Cathedral of the Immaculate Conception was consecrated in 1888. In 1841, the Pope had decreed that the Hong Kong Mission should be kept under Rome's control. Thus the colony became an Italian mission district, and when the Japanese occupied Hong Kong in 1941, the Italian diocese was unharmed because Japan was not at war with Italy. As a result, the cathedral's archives and artefacts have survived better than those of many other churches.

Roman Catholic Cathedral
7am–7pm daily
Mass in English at 9.30am every Sun

Zoological and Botanical Gardens ❷

Across from the cathedral, you will find one of the back entrances to the Zoological and Botanical Gardens. The gardens, opened in 1864, are divided by Albany Road. The Zoo sits on the western side of the road and is home to a good collection of birds, including Asian fowl, Mandarin ducks, peacocks, pheasants and a small collection of mammals, mostly primates. There is also a small open-air reptile house featuring snakes and terrapins.

The Botanical Gardens, on the eastern side of Albany Road, overlook Government House, the former residence of the British governors. Because of the proximity to Government House, the gardens are also known in Chinese as *Bing Tau Fa Yuen*, "Military Chief's (i.e. Governor's) Garden". The gardens are home to a number of exotic trees and plants. A series of sloping pathways wind their way around a central formal garden in which a fountain sits on axis with a statue of George VI. Designed by

Botanical Gardens

Gilbert Ledward, the statue was erected to commemorate the centenary of the founding of the colony of Hong Kong. In the early morning, local residents come to the gardens to practise *tai chi*, *qi gong* and other forms of exercise.

Zoological and Botanical Gardens
6am–7pm daily
Admission free
www.lcsd.gov.hk/parks/hkzbg

Did You Know?
After Britain's handover of Hong Kong to China in 1997, the Queen's image was replaced on the Hong Kong coinage by the bauhinia, Hong Kong's national flower. Though a native species, this flower also has a colonial association: its full name is *Bauhinia blakeana*, in honour of Sir Henry Blake, a dedicated botanist who was governor from 1898 to 1903.

Government House  

Leaving the Zoological and Botanical Gardens via the Garden Road exit, turn left onto Upper Albert Road and on your right will be Government House — official residence of the Chief Executive. Until Hong Kong was handed back to the Chinese in 1997, this was the residence and office of the governor. The need for a residence was apparent as early as 1843, but London was reluctant to provide the funds. When work finally started in the late 1840s, it was at such a slow pace that the house wasn't ready till the middle of the next decade. The final building was modest by the standards of the British Far East, but its commanding location on a plateau looking down on the harbour gave it an unmistakable air of authority. It was altered and extended many times over the years and by the 1920s, it had grown from a modest villa to an Anglo-Indian palace. A large annexe, almost as big as the original house, contained a ballroom, a billiard room, a supper room and card and smoking rooms. The structure was severely weakened by the construction of an air raid tunnel in World War II. During the Japanese occupation it was rebuilt by a

Note: Hong Kong Governors
Sir Arthur Kennedy, governor from 1872 to 1877, was the first to invite the Chinese to functions at Government House, which probably explains why he was the only one to have a statue commemorating his memory. One of the colony's least-liked governors was probably Sir William Des Voeux (in office 1887–1891). He was said to have been unwell most of the time and frequently on leave — shooting trips along the Yangtze River seem to have been his favourite mode of recuperation.

26-year-old railway engineer, Seichi Fujimura, and then redecorated by a firm from Osaka, hence the mix of Japanese and Western elements — an unhappy one, to my eye. The gardens were also landscaped by a gardener from Kyoto. Now with the advent of skyscrapers, the house has lost its beautiful view of the harbour. The grounds are not open to the public, except for one Sunday in March each year when the azaleas are in bloom. The gardens are worth visiting — a weeping willow was planted there to ward off the bad *feng shui* supposedly inflicted by the nearby Bank of China Tower.

The Peak ❹

Retrace your steps back to Garden Road and turn left downhill. The Peak Tram Station will be on your right. Started in 1888, the **Peak Tramway**, which was originally known as the Upper Level Tramway, reduced the time to get to the peak from three hours (by sedan chair) to eight minutes. There have been no accidents since its commencement, and the tram has only ever stopped twice, the first time because of World War II, and in 1966 when violent rainstorms washed half the track away.

When people refer to the **Peak**, they usually mean the plateau (standing at 400 metres above sea level) and its surrounding residential area; the actual summit is Victoria Peak, at 552 metres, which can be reached via Mount Austin Road. The Peak has been the most fashionable place to live in Hong Kong since the British moved in. Taipans (company bosses) built lavish summer houses

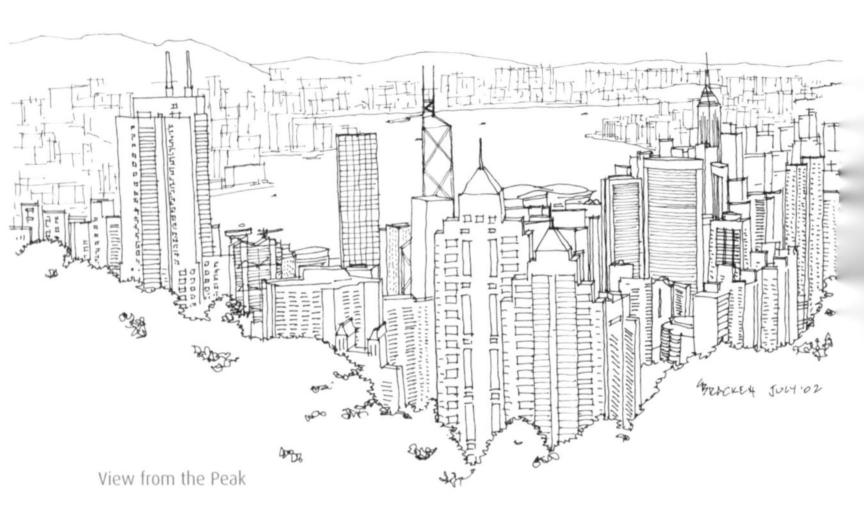

View from the Peak

Did You Know?
In the 1920s, if you missed the last Peak Tram — at 11.45pm — you could hire a private tram at any time up to three in the morning.

there to escape the heat and humidity of the town below. An ordinance in 1904 effectively reserved the whole area for Europeans — the Chinese being kept out by cleverly crafted wording of the building regulations. The view from the Peak is justifiably famous and equally spectacular by day and night.

Victoria Peak Gardens, located near the summit, used to be the grounds of the Governor's mountain lodge, which was burnt down by the Japanese during the occupation. The gardens are open to the public. Observation decks allow views to Victoria Harbour and Kowloon. Harlech Road and Lugard Road are convenient starting points for scenic walks around the Peak. The two roads form a loop about 3.5 km long and are well-lit at night. They also offer an alternative route back down to the city.

The Peak Tram terminus is housed in the **Peak Tower**, built by Terry Farrell and Partners in 1996. In terms of design, the tower seems to fall short of what is expected to complement its spectacular surroundings. Nonetheless, it contains an extensive viewing platform and some restaurants. It sits opposite the even less inspiring Peak Galleria shopping mall.

Hong Kong Park ❺

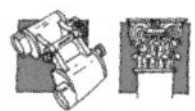

Leave the Peak Tram Station, walk down Cotton Tree Drive and Hong Kong Park will be on your right. Once the grounds of the Victoria Barracks, Hong Kong Park was opened to the public in 1991. Located in the heart of Central and dramatically surrounded by skyscrapers, the park consists of more than 8 hectares of densely wooded land. Mature trees and fine historic buildings, which have been readapted for new uses, can be found scattered throughout. Numerous pedestrian paths link the parts of the city that were previously separated by the barracks. Facilities include an artificial waterfall, fountain plaza, conservatory, aviary, indoor games hall, visual arts centre, playground, observation tower, museum and *tai chi* gardens. The former residence of the Deputy General, Rawlinson House, is now a marriage registry, making the park a popular spot for wedding photo shoots.

Observation Tower,
Hong Kong Park

Perhaps the most remarkable feature of the park is the **Aviary**. Sitting snugly in a steep valley just under Kennedy Road, it houses more than 800 birds as well as a variety of mature trees. Visitors walk along a wooden bridge suspended about 10 metres above the ground, at the level of the tree branches where most of the birds are found. Designed by Wong Tung and Partners in conjunction with Ove Arup and Partners, the enclosing mesh is made up of individual strips of woven stainless-steel wire, supported by a series of hanger bars. The intricacy of the structural components are almost as spectacular as the aviary itself.

Flagstaff House, which houses the **Museum of Teaware**, was constructed in 1846 in the elegant Greek Revival style. Complete with Doric columns and wide verandas well-adapted to the local climate, it was the official residence and office of the Commander of the British Forces up to 1932. In 1984 it was converted into the present museum, showcasing teapots, bowls, trays and other tea paraphernalia from China, some of which date from as far back as the Warring States period (473–221 BC). The Lock Cha Tea House in the adjoining K.S. Lo Gallery serves tea and dim sum in a traditional setting.

Museum of Teaware (Flagstaff House)

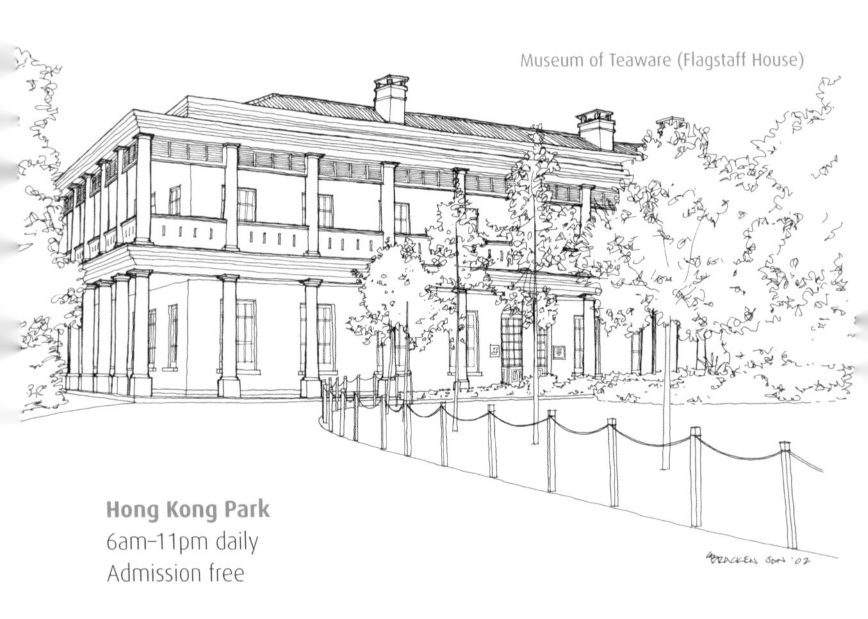

Hong Kong Park
6am–11pm daily
Admission free

Aviary
9am–5pm daily
Admission charges

Museum of Teaware (Flagstaff House)
10am–5pm Wed–Mon
Admission free
Tel: 2869 0690

St John's Cathedral ❻

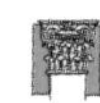

Leave Hong Kong Park via Cotton Tree Drive and follow the small road between Murray Building and Citibank Plaza. You will see St John's Cathedral across Garden Road, its architecture a mixture of Gothic and Romanesque styles. Built in 1847 and consecrated in 1849, this is the oldest Anglican church in East Asia. During the Japanese occupation, the Japanese army transformed the cathedral into their social club, removing the stained-glass windows, the choir stalls and the altar to make room for their activities. After the war, the wooden front doors were rebuilt using timber salvaged from the HMS *Tamar* — the British warship that guarded the entrance to Victoria Harbour — and the stained-glass east window was restored by the workshops of William Morris. The North window is dedicated to those who lost their lives at sea during the two World Wars.

St John's Cathedral
7am–6pm daily
Admission free

French Mission Building (former)

French Mission Building (former)  

Located just behind St John's Cathedral, at No. 8 Garden Road, is the former French Mission Building. This attractive edifice, declared a monument in 1989, is in a very light-handed Neoclassical style. Completed in 1868, it was initially used as the headquarters for the American trading firm Heard & Co; from the 1880s it served as the Russian consulate, and then in 1915 it was bought by the Paris Foreign Missions Society and remodelled. The government bought back the building in 1953, and since then it has been home to a variety of uses, most recently as the Court of Final Appeal.

Bishop's House ❽ 

Walk back out onto Garden Road past the cathedral, turn right, then right again onto Lower Albert Road. Follow it to the very end and you will see the Bishop's House behind a high wall on the left at No. 1 Lower Albert Road. Built in 1848 to accommodate St Paul's College, and as a home for George Smith, the colony's first Anglican bishop, this is reputed to be the second oldest residence in Hong Kong (Flagstaff House is slightly older). Unlike Flagstaff House, this is still inhabited by the functionary it was built for, in this case the Anglican bishop of Hong Kong. Built on a steep, sharp corner of Lower Albert Road, this tall, Gothic house is well-maintained and quite attractive.

Duddell Street ❾

Take the sharp, right-hand turn onto Ice House Street and Duddell Street will be on your left. It is easily recognised, marked by a wide staircase flanked by handsome lamps. Hong Kong in its early years was a dangerous place: it had a largely transient population and was under-policed. In 1847, a law was passed obliging all Europeans to hang lanterns outside their homes in an effort to light the streets. In 1856, oil street lamps were placed on all major thoroughfares. These were replaced by gas lamps from 1864 onwards. By the end of the 19th century, electric street lights were replacing the gas ones. The four lamps on Duddell Street were untouched because they were custom-built for the steps and could not be reused elsewhere. In 1979, they were declared monuments. Since then, the Hong Kong and China Gas Company has generously supplied the gas for free. George Duddell was at one time the third-largest landowner in Hong Kong, and the first Master of Auction. In 1845, he successfully bid for Hong Kong's opium monopoly.

Duddell Street

> **Did You Know?**
> Ice House Street is named for the ice depot that used to be located here. The first shipments of ice arrived in 1847 — all the way from the Great Lakes region of the United States.

Link to the Central walk: Walk to the end of Duddell Street and you will come to Queen's Road Central.

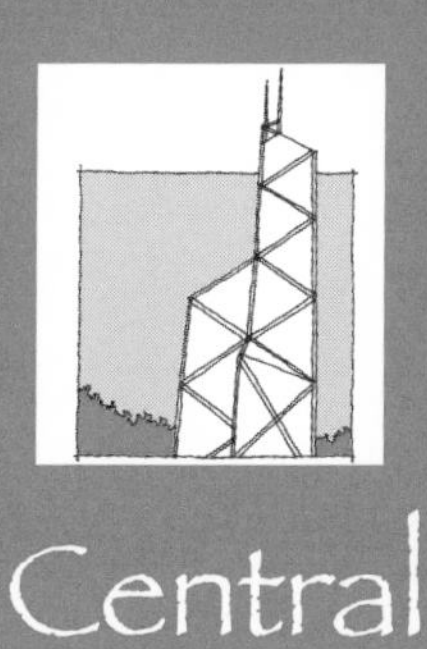

Central

Nearest MTR: Central
Approximate walking time: 1 hour

Central

Central is the business hub of Hong Kong and home to many of Asia's leading banks, trading companies and brokers. Numerous upmarket shopping malls can also be found here, notably the Landmark and the charming, old-world Pedder Building. Central is also where you will find some of Hong Kong's most impressive architecture, such as the historical Old Supreme Court Building, HSBC and the Bank of China Tower.

CENTRAL

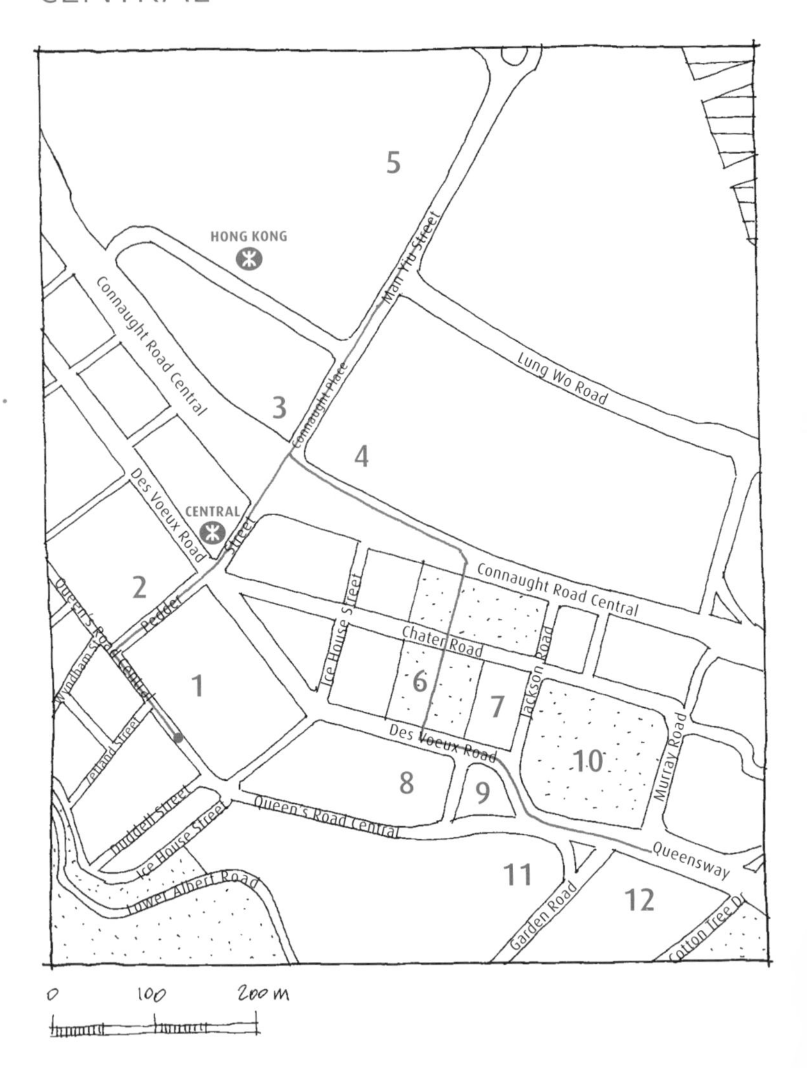

5
HONG KONG
Man Yiu Street
Connaught Road Central
Lung Wo Road
3
Connaught Place
4
Des Voeux Road
CENTRAL
Pedder Street
2
Connaught Road Central
Queen's Road Central
Ice House Street
Chater Road
Jackson Road
1
6
7
Wyndham Street
Zetland Street
Des Voeux Road
10
Murray Road
8
9
Duddell Street
Ice House Street
Queen's Road Central
Queensway
11
Lower Albert Road
Garden Road
12
Cotton Tree Dr
0
100
200 m

KEY

1. The Landmark
2. Pedder Building
3. Exchange Square
4. Jardine House
5. International Finance Centre
6. Statue Square
7. Old Supreme Court Building
8. HSBC
9. Bank of China (former)
10. Chater Gardens
11. Cheung Kong Centre
12. Bank of China Tower

The Landmark ❶

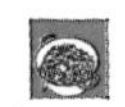 

This upmarket shopping centre, occupying the entire city block between Queen's Road Central and Des Voeux Road Central, is one of the largest in this part of town. Its six storeys are home to some of the world's most renowned brands, including a four-storey Harvey Nichols department store. These shops are arrayed around an enormous atrium and connected to neighbouring buildings via a warren of walkways. The complex also houses the exclusive Landmark Mandarin Oriental Hotel.

Queen's Road Central

Pedder Building ❷

Walk along Queen's Road Central and turn right onto Pedder Street. Pedder Building will be on your left at No. 12. An attractive narrow stone frontage sets it apart from the rest of an architecturally uninteresting street, and leads into a surprisingly spacious interior. Built in 1923, this is the oldest surviving commercial building in Hong Kong, and since 1981 has been listed as a Grade II Historic Building.

Exchange Square ❸

Continue along Pedder Street and cross Connaught Road Central onto Connaught Place. On your left will be Exchange Square, home of the Unified Hong Kong Stock Exchange. Designed by Remo Riva with a team from Palmer and Turner, the building is cladded in bands of pink granite and silver reflective glass, and is most impressive from a distance, particularly from the cross-harbour ferry. The complex consists of two 52-storey office towers, housing

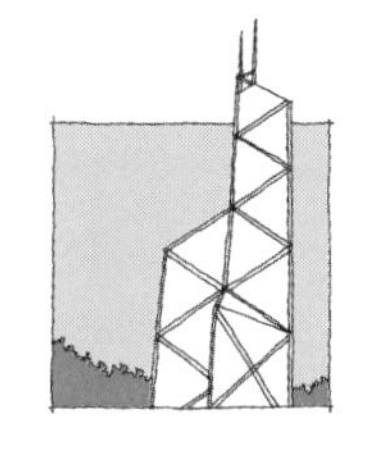

some of the most sought-after office space in the city. Luxury penthouses with private terraces overlooking the harbour are also highly valued. A bus terminus occupies the ground level, with a landscaped public plaza above it, allowing the plaza to be more accessible from the public elevated walkway that runs through this part of Central. Some impressive artworks are to be found here, including a sculpture by Henry Moore that dominates the entrance area and bronzes by Dame Elizabeth Frink, such as the Water Buffalo. The main entrance lobby offers a wonderful view across the harbour to Kowloon.

Jardine House ❹

Across Connaught Place from Exchange Square is Jardine House. Originally known as Connaught Centre, this 52-storey tower was the tallest in Asia when it was built. The site was then on newly reclaimed land and was the most expensive real estate in the world. The developers were keen to come up with a strong architectural icon as well as rentable office space. With its distinctive array of round porthole windows, it became something of an icon for Hong Kong during the 1970s — even as it was unflatteringly nicknamed "Thousand Arseholes" by the Chinese! The fenestration design was in fact influenced by having to build as structurally efficient a building as possible on the soft reclaimed land: circular openings, compared with rectilinear openings, made the building lighter, yet no less strong, and were hence ideal.

International Finance Centre ❺

This complex consists of a vast shopping complex and two office towers, one of which, IFC 2, has become a city landmark because of its sheer size and presence. The elegantly tapering tower was designed by Cesar Pelli and was Hong Kong's tallest building from 2003 to 2010 until overtaken by the International Commerce Centre (ICC) across the harbour. There is no observation deck, but the tower does have some pleasant bars and restaurants on the fifth floor with outdoor terraces. In the basement, the Airport Express terminal is where one may check in and drop off one's bags before going to the airport.

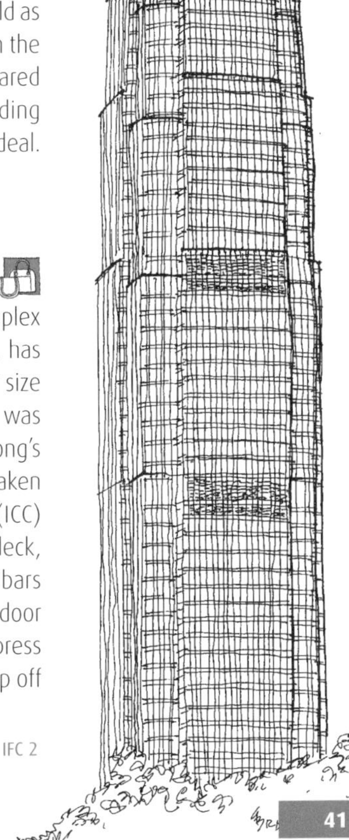

IFC 2

Statue Square 6

Across Connaught Road Central from Jardine House is Statue Square, which takes its name from the statues — mostly of past members of Britain's royal family — which once stood here. The Japanese removed them during the occupation. The sole surviving statue is of Sir Thomas Jackson, a financial head of the Hong Kong and Shanghai Banking Corporation at the end of the 19th century. The **Cenotaph**, an elegantly understated stone monument commemorating Hong Kongers killed in the two World Wars, sits in front of the **Hong Kong Club**, an indifferent-looking office building, home of the once-grandiose club that dominated the waterfront and the colony's social life. All that remains of the original building is an arched entranceway — displayed in the present lobby.

Cenotaph, Statue Square

> **Note: Central on Sunday**
> The streets around Statue Square are closed to traffic on Sundays to allow for the large numbers of foreign domestic workers who work in Hong Kong to get together on their day off. Every inch of pavement between HSBC, Chater Gardens and Exchange Square is taken up by the women chatting, eating, playing games and catching up. The sheer scale of this weekly event has to be seen to be believed.

Old Supreme Court Building

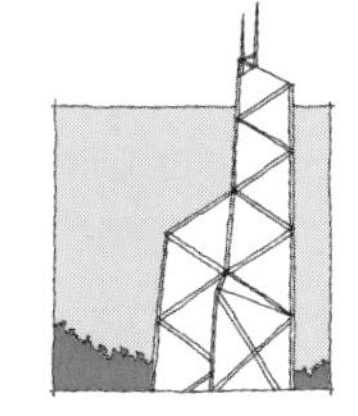

Old Supreme Court Building ❼

Facing onto Statue Square is the Old Supreme Court Building, which served as the home of the highest court in Hong Kong from 1912 to 1985, and subsequently as the Legislative Council Building until 2011. The architecture consists of arcades and loggias of grey granite and Ionic columns topped by the traditional depiction of Justice above the main portico — a blindfolded lady holding a pair of scales in one hand and a sword in the other. The roof has a hint of Chinese architecture. The building's architect, Aston Webb, was also involved in the design of London's Victoria and Albert Museum, as well as the iconic east front of Buckingham Palace.

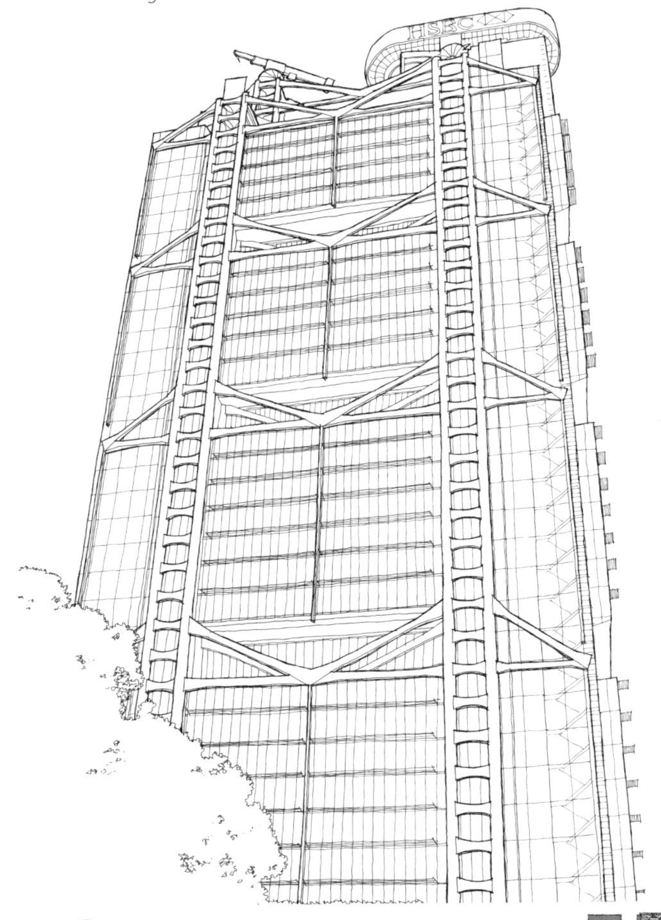

HSBC ❽

HSBC, facing out over Statue Square, is widely regarded as one of the key buildings of the late 20th century. At the time it was built (the early 1980s), it was seen as a much-needed symbol of the bank's confidence in the future of Hong Kong — which was anything but clear. It is actually the fourth HSBC building to stand at No. 1 Queen's Road since the bank's founding in 1865. Construction cost nearly US$1 billion, making it the most expensive building in the world when it was completed in 1985. The design brief required that the original banking hall remain intact throughout the construction process. Architect Norman Foster therefore decided to have the structure hang over the hall from five huge trusses supported by eight groups of four-column steel clusters. This ground-breaking technique eliminated the need for a central core, allowing for a light-filled atrium. Further natural illumination is supplied by the "sun scoop" — 480 computer-controlled mirrors hanging on the south side of the building — which reflects natural light into the heart of the atrium. Almost every component of the building was designed from scratch. The workings of the escalators and lifts are also visible and the stairwells are walled in glass, allowing for stunning views.

The pedestrian plaza beneath the building is most unusual, doing away with the traditional grand entrance. It is said to be designed in the interests of *feng shui*; the escalators were also positioned to maximize the flow of *qi* (positive energy) into the building. It really is worth taking the escalators up into the banking halls to see the 52-metre-high atrium and experience the almost cathedral-like atmosphere in this most extraordinary of corporate headquarters.

Note: HSBC

Known to locals simply as "The Bank", HSBC is listed as the second most profitable public company in Hong Kong. The Hong Kong and Shanghai Banking Corporation was founded in 1865 with a capital of $5 million by an association of local firms and rapidly took a lead in the commercial and industrial life of Hong Kong, and later throughout the Far East. It financed a large percentage of Japan's foreign trade and was responsible for much of the railway development in China.

Bank of China (former) ❾

Across from HSBC sits the former Bank of China, an attractive stone-faced Art Deco-style building dating from 1950. Its facades sit well in relation to the various streets flowing at an assortment of angles around the building. It is now completely dwarfed by its neighbours, particularly the newer Bank of China Tower, but was originally one of the tallest buildings in the Territory. When the Bank of China decided that it had outgrown these premises, they decided to relocate rather than knock down the existing building. The top three floors of this building, once the meeting place of the economic section of the Communist Party, are now home to the exclusive China Club, an elegant rendezvous for Hong Kong's elite modelled after the clubs in pre-war Shanghai. The club houses a members-only restaurant as well as an impressive collection of modern Chinese art.

Bank of China (former)

Chater Gardens ⑩

Diagonally across Des Voeux Road from the former Bank of China is Chater Gardens. The Hong Kong Cricket Club was established here in 1851 before it moved in 1975 to Happy Valley. It was named after Sir Paul Chater, an Armenian financier and philanthropist and, by all accounts, a keen cricketer. It is a remarkably quiet park for such a busy location. In fact, it is a miracle the park has survived at all. Full of shaded, winding walkways and home to a large variety of exotic plants, it is a pleasant place to stroll in. The noise from the surrounding traffic is drowned out by the park's large waterfall.

Did You Know?
Hong Kong, unlike any other British colony, seems to honour it financiers and bankers with statues and gardens more than its military and political leaders.

Bank of China Tower (left) and Cheung Kong Centre (right)

Cheung Kong Centre ⑪

Across Queen's Road Central from Chater Gardens is Cheung Kong Centre. The building stands where the Hilton Hotel used to be and was commissioned by Hong Kong tycoon Li Ka-shing as the headquarters for his Cheung Kong Group. Architects Cesar Pelli and Leo A. Daly seem to have deliberately designed a very plain tower since it is located between two of Hong Kong's architectural icons — HSBC and the Bank of China Tower.

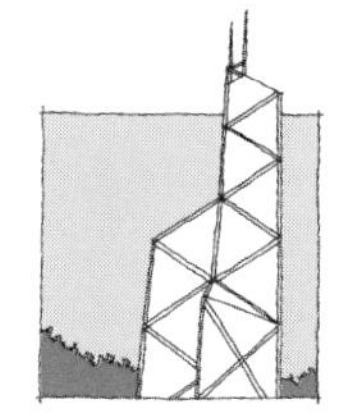

Bank of China Tower ⓬

Across Garden Road from the Cheung Kong Centre sits the Bank of China Tower. Completed in 1990, this building, by its sheer size and architectural presence, makes it perfectly clear who the new power is in town, dwarfing even the nearby HSBC. Designed to withstand typhoon-intensity winds, the building takes its inspiration from the structure of bamboo, which is in effect a sturdy, flexible tube with its strength in its outer walls. The finished building looks nothing like bamboo but works on its structural principle. There are no internal structural columns; vertical loads are diverted to the diagonal cross-braces on the outer walls, thereby reducing the quantity of steel needed by almost half compared to the steel needed for a conventional building of similar height. The form of the tower emerges from a square base that rises and divides into four triangles terminating at different heights and capped with glass roofs. Many locals see the building as a glaring violation of the principles of *feng shui*, what with its triangular prisms in plan, the huge crosses on the sides, and its overall shape resembling a praying mantis. The bad *feng shui* it generates is supposed to be affecting Government House nearby. Express lifts travel to the 42nd floor where visitors get to enjoy panoramic views of Hong Kong.

Slightly further up Garden Road from the Bank of China is **Citibank Plaza**. The site for this building was the last major piece of virgin land in Central. It was initially better known by its lot number, 8888. A prominent local firm, Rocco Design Architects, won the prestigious commission to build here in 1992. The asymmetrical curves of the two office towers rising 40 and 50 storeys form a distinct L-shape and reinforce the building's individuality when seen against the stark geometric lines of the Bank of China Tower.

Bank of China Tower Observation Deck (42nd floor)
9am–6pm Mon–Fri; 9am–1pm Sat
Admission free

Note: Feng Shui
Feng shui is the art of maintaining harmony between man and nature by placing objects in a room or landscape to ensure well-being. It is mainly concerned with location, colour and orientation, and virtually no Hong Konger will ignore its precepts. You will often see small mirrors hanging outside shops and houses — placed there to ward off evil spirits.

Link to Wan Chai walk: Leave Citibank Plaza and turn right down Garden Road, then turn right onto Queensway.

Wan Chai

Nearest MTR: Admiralty
Approximate walking time: 1 hour

Wan Chai

Wan Chai means "Little Bay" in Cantonese because Queen's Road East originally ran along the waterfront — until land reclamation pushed it well inland. Wan Chai is one of Hong Kong's most famous nightlife districts: the area between Hennessy Road and Gloucester Road is famous for its bars, while Jaffe Road and Lockhart Road are known for their many restaurants and clubs. This is an interesting district to explore, with its many street markets, ancient temples and colonial streets such as Johnston Road. Architectural gems include the former Wan Chai Post Office and The Pawn restaurant and bar. The area is also home to higher-end cultural activities, to be found at the Hong Kong Academy for Performing Arts, the Hong Kong Arts Centre and the enormous Hong Kong Convention and Exhibition Centre.

WAN CHAI

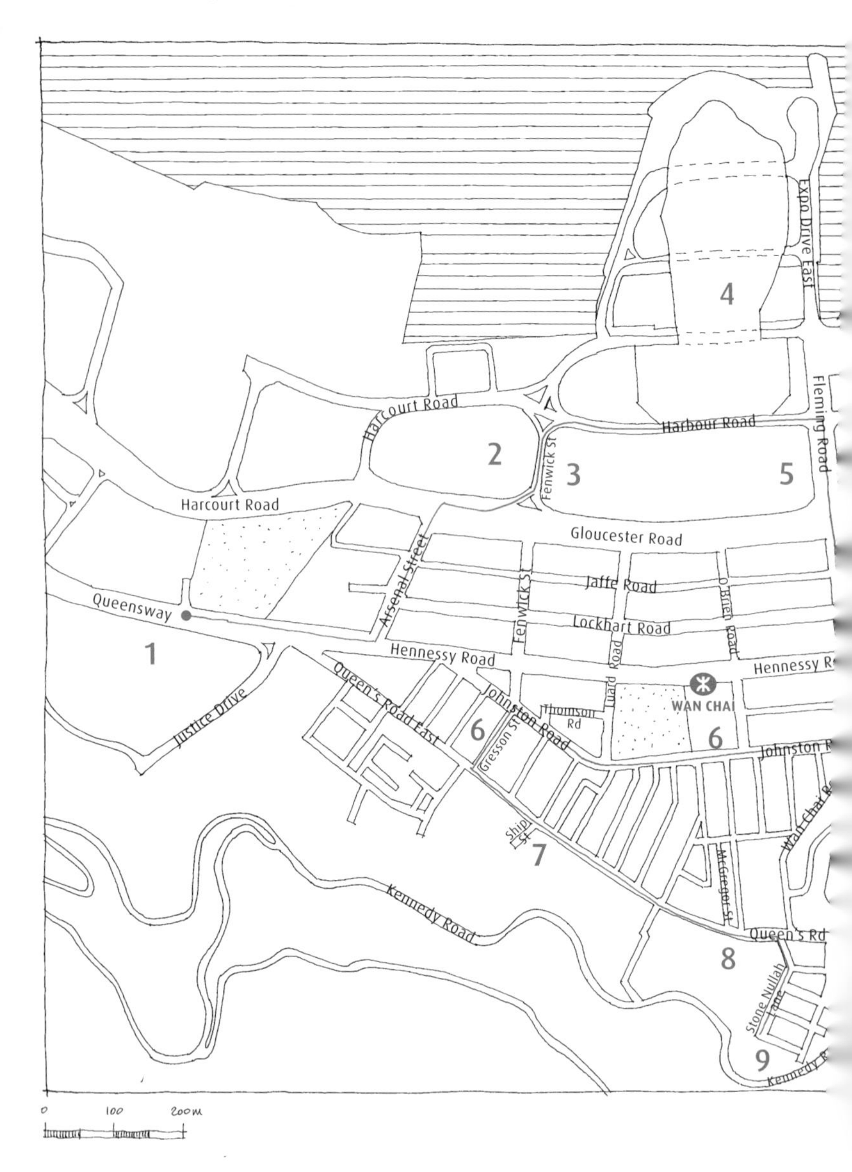

Expo Drive East
4
Fleming Road
Harcourt Road
Harbour Road
2
Fenwick St
3
5
Harcourt Road
Gloucester Road
Arsenal Street
Jaffe Road
O'Brien Road
Fenwick St
Lockhart Road
Queensway
Hennessy Road
Luard Road
Hennessy R
1
Queen's Road East
Johnston Road
Thomson Rd
WAN CHAI
Justice Drive
6
Gresson St
6
Johnston R
Wan Chai R
Ship St
7
McGregor St
Kennedy Road
Queen's Rd
8
Stone Nullah Lane
9
Kennedy R
0
100
200m

KEY

1. Pacific Place
2. Hong Kong Academy for Performing Arts
3. Hong Kong Arts Centre
4. Hong Kong Convention and Exhibition Centre
5. Central Plaza
6. Johnston Road
7. Hung Shing Temple
8. Wan Chai Post Office (former)
9. Pak Tai Temple

Pacific Place ❶

This development was originally part of the massive Victoria Barracks. When the British armed forces began to withdraw in the early 1980s, the area was acquired by Swire Properties and divided into four separate lots: two went to make up Pacific Place, one became Hong Kong Park and the last was used for the new Supreme Court (now High Court). Pacific Place is one of the city's most popular shopping centres and is home to two office towers and three hotels. Designed and constructed in two phases by Wong and Ouyang Ltd, the first phase had to be designed without knowing if the second phase would materialize. In fact, construction began before the whole site had even been bought. The steepness of the site also had to be considered, there being a 26-metre difference between some levels. When graves were discovered on the construction site, Taoist priests had to be called in to perform exorcisms. Despite all these complications, the entire complex has a coherent feel, reinforced by the building's uniform reflective glass walls and white-metal horizontal banding. The changes in level seem natural and the interior is pleasant and bright with clean, simple lines. In the design of the office towers, the architects cleverly gave the building a zig-zag profile to create more corner offices.

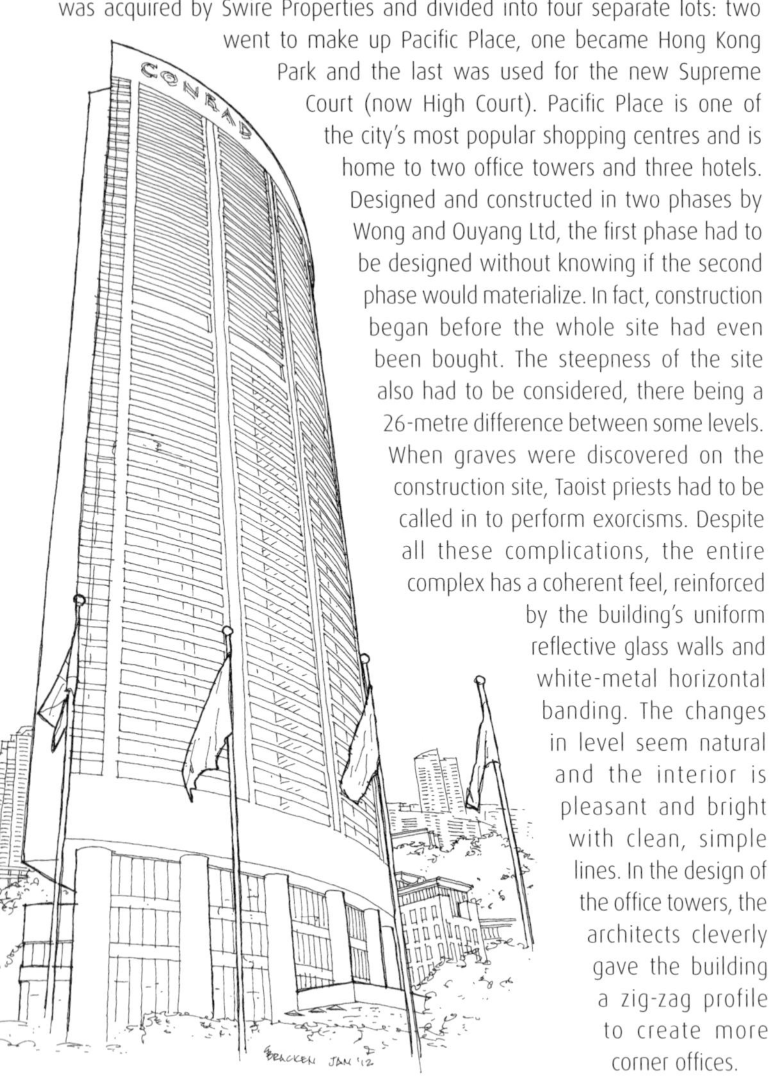

Conrad Hotel, Pacific Place

Did You Know?
It cost approximately US$3 million to preserve a 120-year-old banyan tree at Pacific Place over the five years of construction.

Hong Kong Academy for Performing Arts ❷

Exit Pacific Place and turn right onto Queensway, then left onto Arsenal Street. The Hong Kong Academy for Performing Arts will be at the end of the street, on the other side of Gloucester Road. Completed in 1985, it houses various schools for drama, music, dancing and theatre technology as well as recording halls, television studios and a 1200-seat theatre. The site for this distinctive but somewhat dated-looking building was made up of triangular plots divided by services such as an underground railway line, water supply pipes and sewage reserves. The architects, Simon Kwan and Associates Ltd, cleverly worked around these intrusions, creating a dramatic building with a heavily textured stone-tile cladding.

Hong Kong Academy for Performing Arts
7.30am–11.30pm Mon–Sat
Box office: Noon–6pm Mon–Sat
(self-service ticketing available)
www.hkapa.edu
Tel: 2584 8500

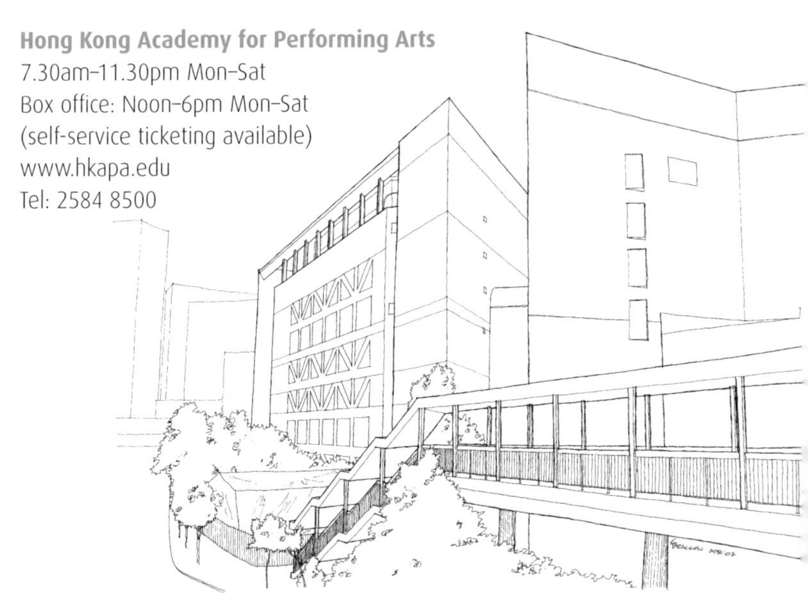

Hong Kong Academy for Performing Arts

Hong Kong Arts Centre ❸

Across Fenwick Street from the Hong Kong Academy for Performing Arts sits the Hong Kong Arts Centre, its entrance at No. 2 Harbour Road. The Hong Kong government granted this small site for the building, but was unwilling to fund the project. In 1977, Tao Ho Design Architects designed a multi-purpose building where the rent from the top seven floors of offices could pay for the construction and upkeep of the arts centre below. The site was sandwiched between two large buildings, making windows or access-ways impossible from those two sides. The architects designed an L-shaped service core with the spaces related to the arts centre stacked on top of each other around a 5-storey atrium. A massive air-conditioning duct currently runs through the atrium-cum-exhibition space as if it were also a display.

Hong Kong Arts Centre
10am–8pm daily
Box office: 10am–6pm daily
Admission free
www.hkac.org.hk
Tel: 2582 0200

Hong Kong Convention and Exhibition Centre ❹

Leave the Hong Kong Arts Centre, turn right onto Harbour Road, and you will come to the Hong Kong Convention and Exhibition Centre soaring above you on your left. Completed just in time to host the 1997 Handover, this convention and exhibition centre was an extension of an existing one. It is built on a spur of reclaimed land that juts into Victoria Harbour and contains three large exhibition halls and a 30-metre-high wall of glass that allows for 180-degree views of the harbour. Skidmore, Owings and Merrill, in conjunction with Wong and Ouyang, designed the free-form roof, which is supposed to resemble a bird in flight.

Running around the periphery of the Convention and Exhibition Centre is a waterfront **Promenade**, along which two commemorative statues can be found. The Reunification Monument is an imposing obelisk that celebrates the Territory's return to China, while the much-smaller Forever Blooming Bauhinia sculpture represents Hong Kong's national emblem.

Hong Kong Convention and Exhibition Centre
9am–7pm daily (may vary)
Admission free, except for certain exhibitions
www.hkcec.com

Central Plaza ❺

Leave the Hong Kong Convention and Exhibition Centre via the elevated pedestrian walkway and follow the signs to Central Plaza (in the direction of Wan Chai MTR station). Central Plaza, at 374 metres, is the third-tallest tower in the city (after IFC 2 and the International Commerce Centre). Originally planned as a 92-storey building, financial constraints resulted in

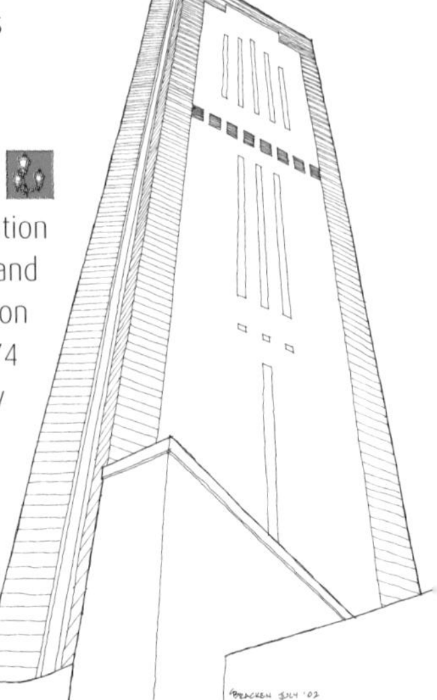

Central Plaza

only 78 storeys being built. The facade is a bit bland and tries to make up for it by having gold and silver ornamental treatment and flashing light displays at night. Even so, it is still not one of the city's most beautiful buildings. There is a sky lobby on the 46th floor open to the public.

Johnston Road 6

Leaving Central Plaza, turn left on Gloucester Road and make an immediate right onto Fleming Road. Follow it until you get to Johnston Road, then turn right. Wan Chai is an area that has retained more of its original character than most other parts of Hong Kong, and Johnston Road is one of the best examples of what the area used to look like before the rampant redevelopment of the 1980s. There are even some of the old shophouses still here, including the imaginatively restored No. 62 Johnston Road, which is now home to **The Pawn**, an upmarket bar and restaurant housed in a gently curving row of narrow, four-storey shophouses dating from the end of the 19th century. Each of the upper floors has a balcony terrace where it is possible to sip drinks or enjoy a meal and catch a flavour of a Hong Kong that has all but vanished.

The warren of narrow streets between Johnston Road and Queen's Road East are vibrant hives of traditional Chinese life. The outdoor market stalls of **Gresson Street** sell all manner of goods, from electronics to birds. The stalls themselves are delicate contraptions of bamboo and steel, often on wheels, and sheltered by colourful striped plastic, with wares dangling precariously from every available space. Temporary, but with an almost sculptural beauty, the stalls are a particularly vibrant form of architecture that seem to perfectly capture the frenetic pace of Hong Kong street

The Pawn

Market, Gresson Street

life. You can find numerous stalls selling hearty Chinese food with plastic tables and chairs balanced on the edge of the pavement. It is common to see shoppers gathering round the back of open vans and trucks bargaining for goods. Behind the crowds stand the traditional crafts shops guarded by mini-shrines surrounded with smouldering joss sticks. It is almost startling to see that the modern city still has such pockets of old-world charm flourishing in the narrow chasms between skyscrapers.

Note: Trams

Taking one of Hong Kong's double-decker trams is not only an excellent way of seeing the city but also good fun and cheap. When the first tram line — which ran from Kennedy Town, at the eastern end of the island, to Shau Kei Wan, in the west — was inaugurated in 1904, it ran through a considerably less urban landscape. It was such a novelty that all the stops were packed with people who just wanted to get on, walk through the carriage and then get off again. There were separate cars for Europeans and those who were known as "natives". The network of tram lines has increased over the years, but most of them still pass through Sheung Wan, Central and Admiralty. Trams mostly run from 6am to midnight daily.

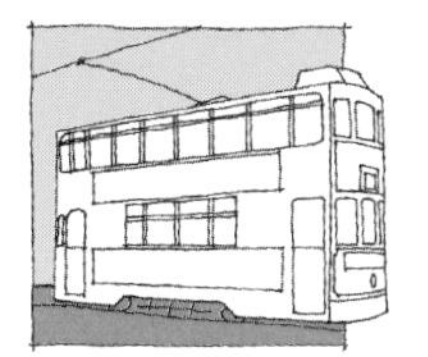

Hung Shing Temple 7

Leave the side streets parallel to Gresson Street, then turn left onto Queen's Road East and you will see the Hung Shing Temple on your right. This richly decorated place of worship is dedicated to Hung Shing (also known as Tai Wong), the God of the Southern Sea. Traditional dragon guards located on each side of the front door are carved as part of the granite beams. In the forecourt is a sacrificial furnace where offerings to the dead can be made, while a 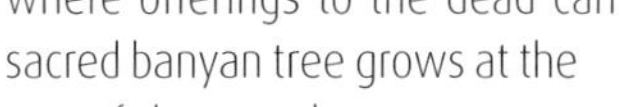 sacred banyan tree grows at the rear of the temple.

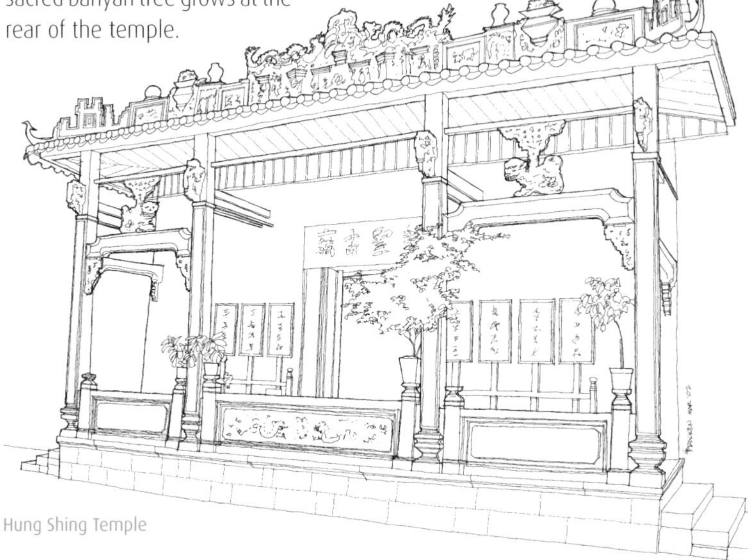

Hung Shing Temple

Wan Chai Post Office (former) 8

Continue along Queen's Road East and the former Wan Chai Post Office will be on your right, at No. 221. This is a tiny but beautifully detailed Edwardian building with a decorative gable over its entrance. Built between 1912 and 1913, it was home to the Wan Chai Post Office until 1992. Fortunately, it was saved from destruction, and a number of its original fittings have been preserved. The building now houses an Environmental Resource Centre run by the Environmental Protection Department which is open to the public.

Pak Tai Temple 9

Continue along Queen's Road East and take the next right onto Stone Nullah Lane. Follow the lane until you see the Pak Tai Temple on your right. This Taoist temple was built in the 1860s and is dedicated to the god Pak Tai ("Northern Emperor"), a deity with powers of subduing disasters and maintaining peace. A 3m-high statue of him, made in the early 17th century, can be found inside sitting on a throne. Around it are figures representing soldiers and

Wan Chai Post Office (former)

scholars. This temple, like all Taoist places of worship, has no set times for services. Instead worshippers come when the feeling moves them to pray and to make offerings. The best view of the temple is from Kennedy Road, which can be accessed via the broad staircase behind the temple at the end of Stone Nullah Lane.

Link to Causeway Bay walk: Retrace your steps down Stone Nullah Lane and turn right onto Queen's Road East. Follow it to the end before turning right onto Wong Nai Chung Road. Turn right again onto Hau Tak Lane and the Sikh Temple will be at the end of the lane on your right.

Pak Tai Temple

Causeway Bay

Nearest MTR: Causeway Bay
Approximate walking time: 1 hour 30 minutes

Causeway Bay

This was the location of the original settlement of Hong Kong until malaria outbreaks forced the early settlers to move elsewhere. The area has since become the centre for sporting life, exemplified by its famous racecourse, Victoria Park and the yacht harbour. Causeway Bay is a haven for shoppers, with vibrant streets such as Jardine's Bazaar and Jardine's Crescent. Historic finds within the area include temples and cemeteries dating back to the founding of the colony, and the daily firing of the Noonday Gun.

CAUSEWAY BAY

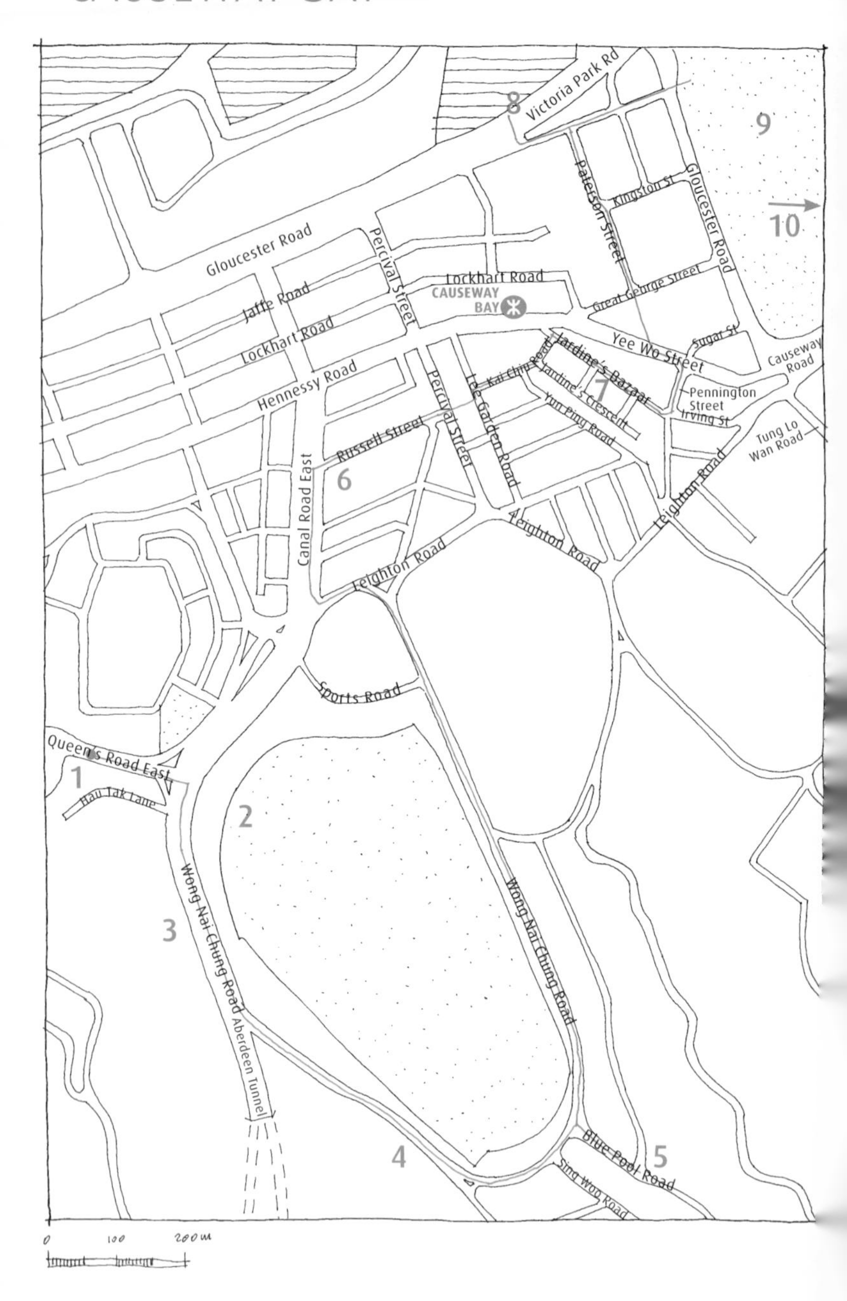

KEY

1. Sikh Temple
2. Happy Valley Racecourse
3. Cemeteries
4. Hindu Temple
5. Tam Kung Temple
6. Times Square
7. Jardine's Bazaar
8. Noonday Gun
9. Victoria Park
10. Tin Hau Temple

Sikh Temple

Sikh Temple ❶

The small, two-storey Khalsa Diwan Sikh Temple lies hidden at the end of Hau Tak Lane, a cul-de-sac near the Happy Valley Racecourse, facing the terraces of the Muslim cemetery. The originally symmetrical facade has lost much of its charm due to insensitive extensions to the building. In the middle of the 19th century, a large number of Sikhs came to Hong Kong from British India to work in the police force. They were ideal candidates for keeping the peace in Hong Kong's unruly streets as they were considered less corrupt than the Chinese, and wouldn't take to drink, unlike many of the early European officers.

Happy Valley Racecourse ❷

Retrace your steps down Hau Tak Lane and the **Hong Kong Jockey Club** will be facing you across Wong Nai Chung Road. Horse races first took place at Happy Valley in the 1840s when the area was a lush, rice-growing valley. Today, the Happy Valley Racecourse, and the newer and larger track at Sha Tin in the New Territories, hold about 75 race meetings a year between them. The racing season runs from September to June, and most races are held on Wednesday nights. A day at the races is a quintessential Hong Kong experience. Visitors staying in Hong Kong less than 21 days can get a tourist ticket, which grants admission even if the racecourse is crowded, as it frequently is. Remember to bring your passport to qualify.

Racing buffs can also learn about racing history at the **Hong Kong Racing Museum**, where eight galleries and a showcase cinema tell the fascinating story of horse racing in Hong Kong. It is conveniently located next to the racecourse on the second floor of the Happy Valley Stand.

Hong Kong Jockey Club

Happy Valley Racecourse
Races September to June, 7–11pm, every Wed and weekends as scheduled
Admission charges
www.happyvalleyracecourse.com

Hong Kong Racing Museum
10am–5pm Tue–Sun
Admission free

> **Did You Know?**
> Hong Kong bets more on horse racing than anywhere else in the world.

Cemeteries ❸

Across Wong Nai Chung Road from the racecourse you will find a series of cemeteries which date from the founding of the colony of Hong Kong. There are Catholic, Protestant, Muslim and Parsee (Zoroastrian) burial grounds. Happy Valley was something of a misnomer because the area was actually a malaria-infested bog — quite a number of the early settlers died and were buried here. Apart from malaria, early Hong Kong was also at risk of getting the bubonic plague until it was discovered that rats and fleas carried it and that proper sanitation would do much to keep it at bay. Even so, as late as 1894, an outbreak killed more than 2500 people, mostly Chinese. Many of those victims were buried here, as were the victims of a huge fire at the racecourse in the 1920s.

In St Michael's Catholic cemetery are a number of Portuguese tombstones that highlight the strong links with nearby Macau. In the Muslim cemetery, there is a surprisingly high number of Chinese names. This particular burial

Parsee Cemetery

ground offers pleasant views of the Sikh Temple on Hau Tak Lane. The Parsee cemetery, dated 1852, is the most beautiful, with well-defined paths opening vistas to mausoleums and beautiful landscapes. There is a Jewish cemetery on nearby Shan Kwong Road — worth a detour to see the memorials of a number of Hong Kong's prominent citizens.

Cemeteries
7am–7pm daily
Admission free

Hindu Temple ❹

Just past the cemeteries and on the same side of Wong Nai Chung Road is a large Hindu temple. Although the facade has been marred by service piping and ducts, it is still possible to discern the form of what must have originally been quite a handsome building. The top floor has a series of large, attractively detailed windows overlooking the racecourse, and an impressive dome sits atop the ensemble. The detailing is unusually restrained for a Hindu temple.

Tam Kung Temple ❺

Continue following Wong Nai Chung Road as it veers to the left around the racecourse and then turn right onto Blue Pool Road. At the corner of the

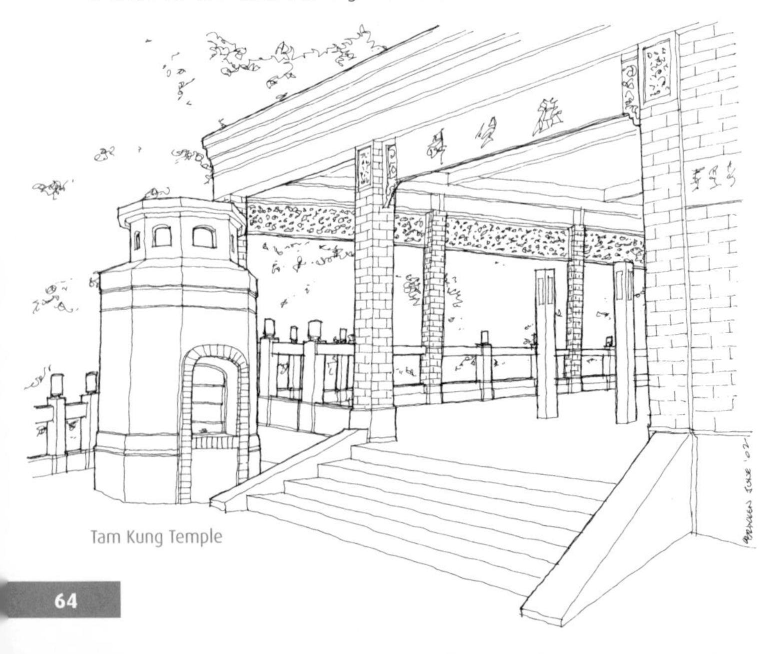

Tam Kung Temple

first street to the left, Ventris Road, you will see the quaint arched gateway of Tam Kung Temple. Once through the red-columned arch, follow the long staircase as it winds its way up to the temple at the top of the hill. The temple itself is a simple structure in brick and plaster which has quite a rural feel. It is surrounded by mature trees and vegetation. A furnace located near the entrance allows the faithful to make their offerings. This is one of the many temples in Hong Kong dedicated to the sea god, Tam Kung.

Tam Kung Temple
8am–5pm daily

Times Square

Times Square ❻

Return to Wong Nai Chung Road and continue along it until the end. Turn left onto Leighton Road, then right onto Canal Road East, and Times Square will be on your right overlooking the junction with Russell Street. This is Causeway Bay's largest mall, with 12 floors all dedicated to the city's favourite pastime: shopping. Times Square is also home to a number of restaurants, cafes and even has a cinema complex. The plaza in front of the Russell Street entrance is often full of street performers. One of Hong Kong's most popular tourist destinations (it gets about 150,000 visitors a day), Times Square sits at the heart of a web of narrow streets that radiate out from the complex, which are particularly good for anyone in search of a bargain in clothing, electronics or jewellery.

Jardine's Bazaar ❼

Walk along Russell Street and cut through to Kai Chiu Road, which veers to the left. Then take a right and you will be on Jardine's Bazaar. Causeway Bay and Happy Valley were the original places of the settlement of Hong Kong. The settlement started when William Jardine, a Scottish trader, and his compatriot partner, James Matheson, decided to build a Chinese district for their workers. Later, due to malaria outbreaks in Happy Valley, the town was re-established in Central. As Hong Kong gradually expanded, this area once again became part of the city. With its docks and warehouses, homes and offices, as well as numerous entertainment places, it was busy around the clock. Today, Jardine's Bazaar and Jardine's Crescent are still lively shopping streets, not particularly upmarket, but interesting enough to be worth a visit.

Jardine's Bazaar

Note: Illegal Facades

Almost anywhere in this part of town, look up and you will see what are known as illegal facades — additions and alterations that pay no heed to building regulations. The shapes of the cantilevered balconies, the patterns of the ornamental grilles, the awnings, the plants, and even the laundry lines are all expressions of the residents' creativity and testaments to their faith in these constructions to actually stay standing. Individual needs, as well as each owner's taste, are all that govern these precarious additions. They occur everywhere in Hong Kong, showing that the real spirit of the place consists in much more than huge, anonymous skyscrapers.

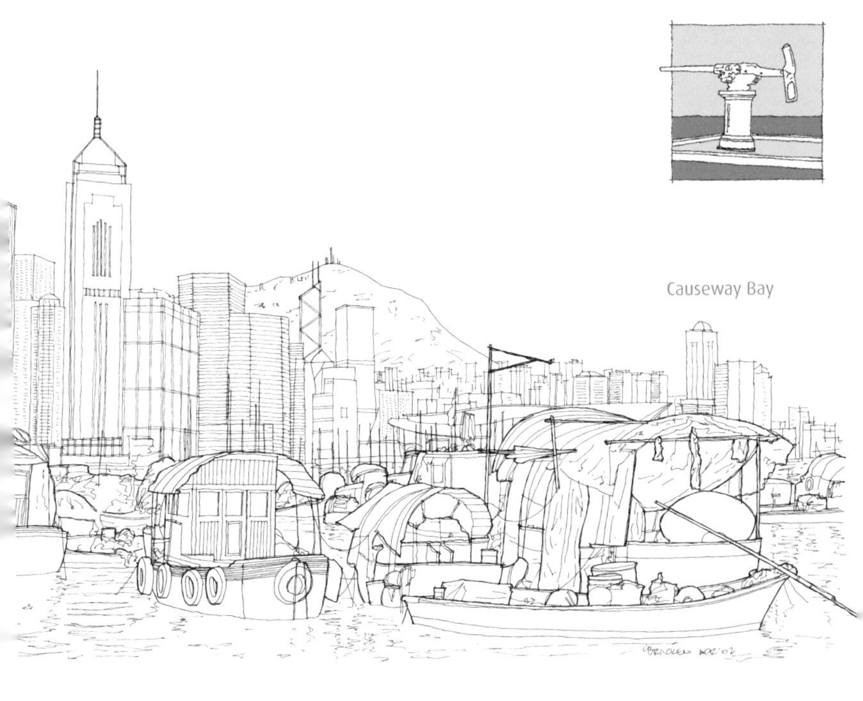

Noonday Gun 8

Leave Jardine's Bazaar by turning left onto Pennington Street. Cross Yee Wo Street (via the circular pedestrian overpass) and follow Patterson Street to the end and you will come out at the Causeway Bay Typhoon Shelter. The Noonday Gun is by the water in front of the Excelsior Hotel. One of the remnants of Hong Kong's colonial past, this Hotchkiss three-pound cannon is dutifully fired at noon every day. It is also fired at midnight during the New Year. The tradition is said to have come about when the British Navy wanted to use up its remaining stock of ammunition and therefore fired one shot every day at noon. Another story has it that there had been a tradition of firing off a salvo as a greeting whenever a senior officer entered the harbour. A more likely explanation is that the Navy used to fire a gun every day at noon to allow ships in the harbour to reset their chronometers. The practice was rendered obsolete in 1885 when the new observatory took over the service of providing the ships in the harbour with daily chronometric readings. However, by that time it had become too much of a popular tradition and hence continues to this day.

The waterfront here used to be crowded with Chinese junks and sampans; these have been joined in recent years by more and more yachts. The western part of Causeway Bay is home to the **Hong Kong Yacht Club**.

Did You Know?

The Noonday Gun is mentioned in Noel Coward's song, Mad Dogs and Englishmen: "In Hong Kong / They strike a gong / And fire off a noonday gun / To reprimand each inmate / Who's in late".

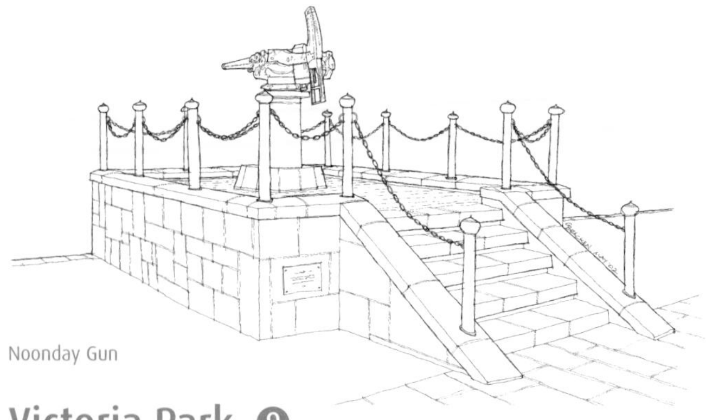
Noonday Gun

Victoria Park ❾

Follow Gloucester Road to the end and you will see Victoria Park ahead of you. Constructed on land reclaimed from what was a typhoon shelter, it is immensely popular, especially in the evenings and on weekends. In the morning you will see throngs of people practising *tai chi*. The park turns into a flower market just before the Chinese New Year (late January or early February). Facilities include an Olympic-size swimming pool (open from April to October), tennis courts, a model-boat pool and a football field.

Tin Hau Temple ❿

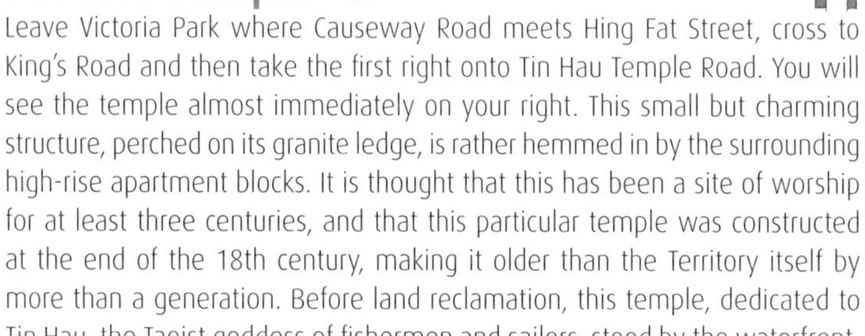

Leave Victoria Park where Causeway Road meets Hing Fat Street, cross to King's Road and then take the first right onto Tin Hau Temple Road. You will see the temple almost immediately on your right. This small but charming structure, perched on its granite ledge, is rather hemmed in by the surrounding high-rise apartment blocks. It is thought that this has been a site of worship for at least three centuries, and that this particular temple was constructed at the end of the 18th century, making it older than the Territory itself by more than a generation. Before land reclamation, this temple, dedicated to Tin Hau, the Taoist goddess of fishermen and sailors, stood by the waterfront.

End of Hong Kong Island walks.

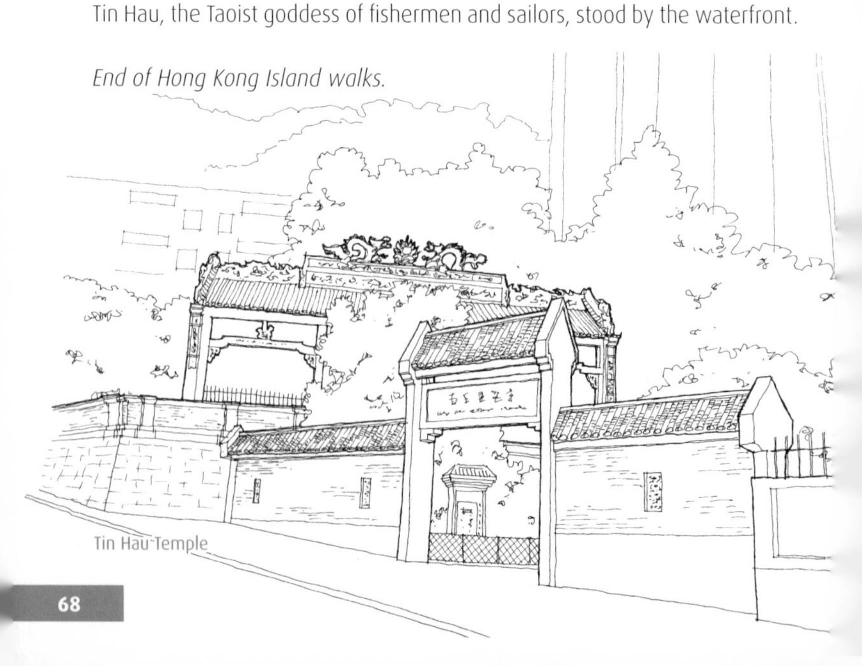
Tin Hau Temple

Kowloon South (Tsim Sha Tsui)

Nearest MTR: Tsim Sha Tsui
Approximate walking time: 1 hour

Kowloon South (Tsim Sha Tsui)

Lying at the southern tip of the Kowloon Peninsula, Tsim Sha Tsui is home to some of Hong Kong's best museums, including the Museum of Art and the Space Museum. These are linked to the Hong Kong Cultural Centre by the spectacular Tsim Sha Tsui Promenade along the waterfront. In this district you will also find the famous Peninsula Hotel, the Marine Police Headquarters and the old railway Clock Tower. Nathan Road is a world-famous shopping street and links the harbour with Kowloon Park, an oasis of greenery at the heart of the bustling district.

KOWLOON SOUTH (TSIM SHA TSUI)

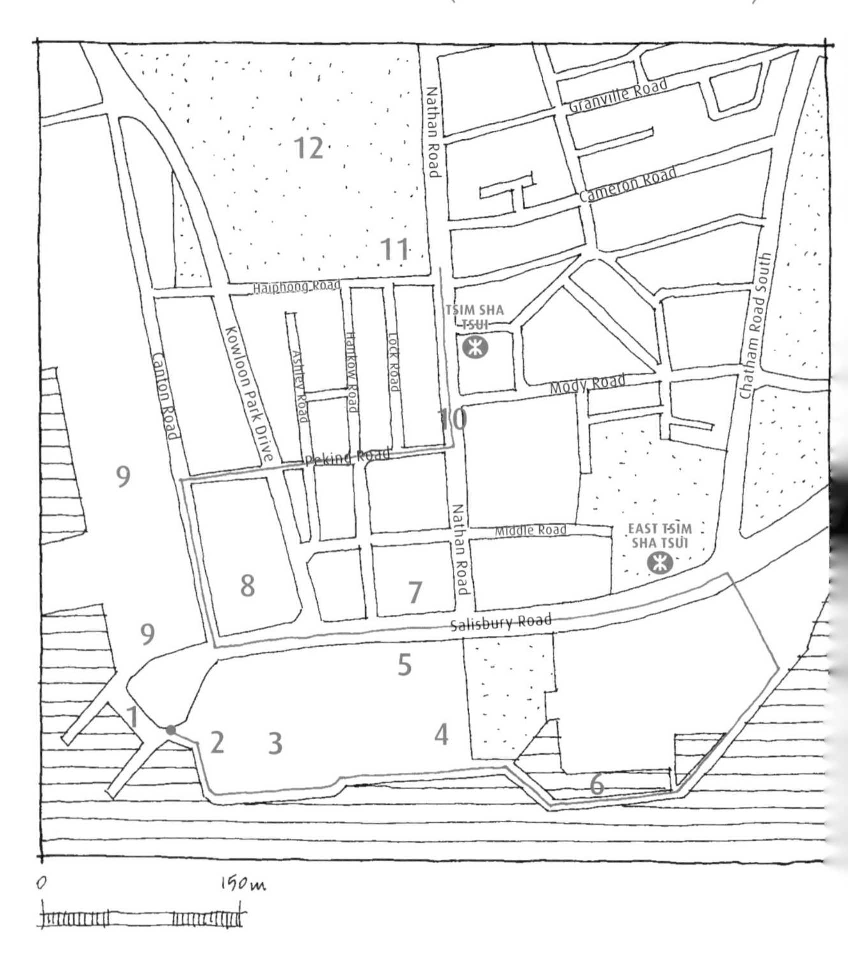

KEY

1. Star Ferry
2. Clock Tower
3. Hong Kong Cultural Centre
4. Hong Kong Museum of Art
5. Hong Kong Space Museum
6. Tsim Sha Tsui Promenade
7. Peninsula Hotel
8. Marine Police Headquarters (former)
9. Star House
10. Nathan Road
11. Kowloon Mosque
12. Kowloon Park

Star Ferry ❶

Since 1888, double-decker ferries have crossed between Hong Kong Island and Kowloon. The journey has become increasingly shorter because of land reclamation narrowing the distance between them. A ride on the ferries ranks as one of the best bargains in Hong Kong, and apart from being good fun, it is an excellent way of seeing one of the most beautiful city harbours in the world. There are four routes, the one between Tsim Sha Tsui and Central being the busiest. The journey takes about seven minutes, and the ferries depart every five or ten minutes. The Star Ferry Pier also contains a **Tourist Information Office**, located just beside the disembarkation point.

Star Ferry
6.30am–11.30pm daily
Fares vary
www.starferry.com.hk

Tourist Information Office
8am–8pm daily

Star Ferry

> **Did You Know?**
> The ferries in the fleet include *Morning Star*, *Northern Star*, *Twinkling Star*, *Golden Star*, and, the oldest among them, *Celestial Star*.

Clock Tower ❷

Leaving the Star Ferry Terminal you will see the 44m-tall Clock Tower straight ahead of you, the last remnant of the Kowloon-Canton Railway Station. Governor Matthew Nathan, after whom Nathan Road is named, was obsessed with railways and wanted to have a link between Canton (now Guangzhou) and Peking (now Beijing). Built in 1916, the resulting railway station was a

Clock Tower

charming Edwardian building. By 1977, however, it had become too small to handle the increasing numbers of passengers and had to be demolished. A campaign by conservationists failed to overturn this decision, but they managed at least to save the clock tower.

Hong Kong Cultural Centre ❸

Immediately behind the Clock Tower is the Hong Kong Cultural Centre, one of Hong Kong's landmark buildings, built on the site formerly occupied by the Kowloon-Canton Railway Station. When plans for the development were initially announced, expectations were understandably high. People were looking forward to a building that would make a statement and best represent Hong Kong and its culture to international ships passing through the harbour. It was to be an icon seen on millions of postcards worldwide. Initially, there were misgivings about the scheme because the building, which faces one of the world's most spectacular views, had no windows. Gradually the public was won over. The main part of the building has a splayed base and an exaggerated pitched roof. It houses a 2000-seat concert hall, a theatre, rehearsal and practice rooms, an exhibition gallery, an art library and a number of restaurants. Any question as to its popularity can be dismissed in that it gets about 800,000 visitors a year. It is also a favourite site for wedding photos because of the city backdrop across the harbour.

Hong Kong Cultural Centre
9am–11pm daily
Box office: 10am–9.30pm daily
Admission free
Tel: 2734 2009

Did You Know?
The pale-pink ceramic tiles used on the exterior walls of the Hong Kong Cultural Centre have invited unflattering comparisons to a giant bathroom!

Hong Kong Museum of Art ❹

The Hong Kong Museum of Art — the largest museum in Hong Kong — sits on the waterfront adjacent to the Hong Kong Cultural Centre. The collection of Chinese art and antiquities is vast and includes ceramics, bronzes, jades and lacquerware. The museum also has exhibits on wall hangings, scrolls and calligraphy, some of which date back to the 16th century. But perhaps the most interesting part of the collection is the clothing section, which showcases the tiny, 3-inch-long shoes that used to be worn by women with bound feet. The Historical Pictures gallery has a large collection of watercolour and oil paintings as well as pencil sketches and lithographs showing life in Hong Kong, Macau and Canton (now Guangzhou) from the late 18th century onwards. The contemporary art selection is perhaps the weakest part of what is otherwise an excellent museum.

Hong Kong Museum of Art
10am–6pm Mon–Wed and Fri; 10am–8pm Sat
Admission charges, but free on Wed
Tel: 2721 0116

Hong Kong Space Museum ❺

The Hong Kong Space Museum is located behind the Museum of Art and overlooks Salisbury Road. Its ball-shaped exterior houses a planetarium, known as the Space Theatre, which screens IMAX films in English and in Cantonese. The complex also houses a Hall of Space Science and a Hall of Astronomy. Exhibits include a piece of moon rock, models of rockets and NASA's 1962 Mercury space capsule.

Hong Kong Space Museum
1–9pm Mon and Wed–Fri; 10am–9pm Sat–Sun and public holidays
Admission charges, but free on Wed
Tel: 2721 0226

Tsim Sha Tsui Promenade ❻

The Tsim Sha Tsui Promenade runs along the southern coast of the Kowloon Peninsula from the Star Ferry Terminal to Hung Hom. This pedestrian path offers some of the best views in Hong Kong, equally stunning by day and by night. It is always busy, particularly during the New Year celebrations, when huge crowds gather to watch the fireworks displays. It's also a good place to watch the dragonboat races every summer.

Part of it is known as the **Avenue of Stars** and features statues of some of Hong Kong and Asia's most famous movie actors, particularly action stars such as Bruce Lee (actually American) and Michelle Yeoh (from Malaysia, the first Asian Bond girl). The Hong Kong stars' names may be less familiar to some but they have huge followings here.

Continue along the Promenade until the end and you will come to Salisbury Road. Signal Hill Garden is across the road, home to the **Blackhead Point Signal Tower**, which was built in 1907 to house the time-ball, a signalling device to allow ships in the harbour to reset their clocks.

Tsim Sha Tsui Promenade
Open 24 hours
Admission free

Blackhead Point Signal Tower
9–11am and 4–6pm daily
Admission free

Central skyline seen from Tsim Sha Tsui Promenade

Peninsula Hotel

Peninsula Hotel ➐

Turn left onto Salisbury Road and you will come to the Peninsula Hotel on your right just after Nathan Road. Opened in 1928, it is Hong Kong's oldest surviving hotel, and its lavish interior is well worth visiting. Before World War II it was one of a very select number of hotels, along with the Raffles in Singapore and the Oriental in Bangkok, which were synonymous with luxury. Japanese troops established their headquarters in the hotel during their occupation, renaming it The Toa. Because of this it was kept in better condition than most of Hong Kong's landmarks and was able to reopen quickly after the war. The hotel is also famous for having the world's largest fleet of Rolls-Royce limousines.

Felix Restaurant, located at the top of the 30-storey extension added in 1995, was designed by Philippe Starck. This is one interior that simply has to be experienced. The dining room is large, with high ceilings, and decorated in typically stripped-down Starck style. Huge glass walls overlook the harbour and the rest of Kowloon. If the price of a dinner makes you reconsider, you can always have a drink at the bar. The restrooms have to be seen to be believed.

Peninsula Hotel
www.peninsula.com
Tel: 2920 2888

Marine Police Headquarters (former) 8

Continue along Salisbury Road and the former Marine Police Headquarters will be on your right. A water police force was set up in 1841 because Hong Kong had for centuries been notorious as a base for pirates; renamed the Marine Police in 1848, it became fully integrated into the regular police force. This elegant, asymmetrical building was built as their headquarters in 1884. It used to overlook the entire harbour but because of recent land reclamation it finds itself well inland. The Japanese used it as their naval headquarters during their occupation. It was declared a historical monument in 1994 and has been imaginatively rejuvenated as **1881 Heritage**, which houses a boutique hotel, an upmarket shopping complex, and several elegant restaurants and bars.

1881 Heritage (former Marine Police Headquarters)

Star House 9

At the end of Salisbury Road, again on the right-hand side, sits the popular Star House shopping complex. This is a good place to buy all kinds of cheap goods, especially electronics. Overlooking the busy plaza interchange in front of the Star Ferry Pier, for which it is named, this is actually a rather unremarkable looking Modernist commercial building built in concrete. It is considerably enlivened, however, by the bustling commercial activity it houses.

Turn onto Canton Road and follow it until you come to **Harbour City** on your left. Canton Road used to be the waterfront until the 1950s, when the land was reclaimed and became home to this vast complex, which includes the adjoining Ocean Terminal and Ocean Centre. Home to more than 700 shops, scores of restaurants as well as three hotels, Harbour City is one of the largest shopping complexes in the city. Ocean Terminal is where all but the very largest luxury liners dock when visiting Hong Kong.

Nathan Road ⑩

Leave Canton Road via Peking Road; follow it and you will come to Nathan Road. When Nathan Road was being constructed in the early 20th century, the governor after whom it was named was derided for having built a road through what was then the unpopulated Kowloon Peninsula. Sir Matthew Nathan became governor at the age of 42 and was the only Jewish governor in Hong Kong's history. Nathan Road runs from the waterfront at the tip of the Kowloon Peninsula all the way to the border with the New Territories and is packed with an amazing mix of shops selling everything from electronics to jewellery to suits, and top-class hotels mingling with seedy guesthouses.

One of the most famous buildings on Nathan Road has to be **Chungking Mansions**, at Nos. 36–44, a dingy-looking, high-rise budget-accommodation ghetto filled with backpackers and immigrants (not all of whom are legal). It was immortalised in Wong Kar Wai's 1994 film, "Chungking Express", which has since become something of a cult classic. The trees that once lined this roadway are long gone, replaced by brash neon lights and garish glittering signage.

Located off Nathan Road (almost opposite Peking Street) is **Mody Road**. Once home to bargain retailers, it now makes for a more fashionable shopping experience and is well worth a stroll.

Did You Know?
Hong Kong's Indian tailors are famous for the speed and quality of their work, although sometimes the customer must be prepared to sacrifice one for the other. Even though the Indian tailors take the measurements, the garments are usually made by Chinese workers.

Kowloon Mosque ⑪

Continue along Nathan Road and you will come to the Kowloon Mosque. Located at the southeast corner of Kowloon Park, where Nathan Road meets Haiphong Road, this is the largest mosque in Hong Kong. It was built in 1984 to replace an older mosque dating from 1896 — at the other end of Kowloon Park — in which Indian-Muslim troops stationed in the barracks worshipped. The Kowloon Mosque is traditional in its form and layout, with a central dome surrounded by minarets. The exterior is cladded simply in white marble. Muslims are welcome to attend prayers, but non-Muslims should ask permission before going inside, and must remove their shoes at the entrance.

Kowloon Mosque

Kowloon Mosque
11am–6pm Thurs; 3–6pm Sat
Tel: 2724 0095

Kowloon Park ⓬

This is one of Hong Kong's most popular parks, with as many as 100,000 people using it every day. Once the site of the Whitfield Barracks for British and Indian troops, it was officially opened as a park in 1970 but really only took off after a massive redevelopment in 1989. It was then reborn as an oasis of green just off one of the busiest sections of Nathan Road. Laid out around a main north-south axis linking the Haiphong Road entrance to the sports complex, walkways criss-cross the park and join the numerous facilities to one another. Areas of interest include a Chinese garden, a maze, a fountain, an adventure

Chinese Garden, Kowloon Park

playground, restaurants and an open-air Sculpture Walk that features works of international artists. The sports complex has a heated indoor Olympic-size swimming pool and sports halls. The reinforced-concrete barrel-vaulted roof that runs the entire length of the building manages to achieve a light and transparent feel. Outside the complex are soccer pitches and volleyball courts.

Kowloon Park
5am–midnight daily
Admission free
www.lcsd.gov.hk/parks/kp

Sports Centre
7am–11pm daily
Admission charges

Swimming Pool
6.30am–10pm daily
Admission charges

Link to Kowloon North (Yau Ma Tei) walk: Leave Kowloon Park and walk along Granville Road until you see the Hong Kong Science Museum ahead of you, across Chatham Road South.

Kowloon North (Yau Ma Tei)

Nearest MTR: Jordan
Approximate walking time: 45 minutes

Kowloon North (Yau Ma Tei)

This part of the Kowloon Peninsula, which runs north from Tsim Sha Tsui in the direction of Boundary Street, is where Hong Kong and China really begin to converge. It has one of the highest population densities in the world and is also one of the city's busiest shopping districts. Particularly noteworthy are the Temple Street Night Market and the Jade Market. Yau Ma Tei is also home to charming colonial buildings, such as the Hong Kong Museum of History and the Old South Kowloon District Court, as well as interesting places of worship.

KOWLOON NORTH (YAU MA TEI)

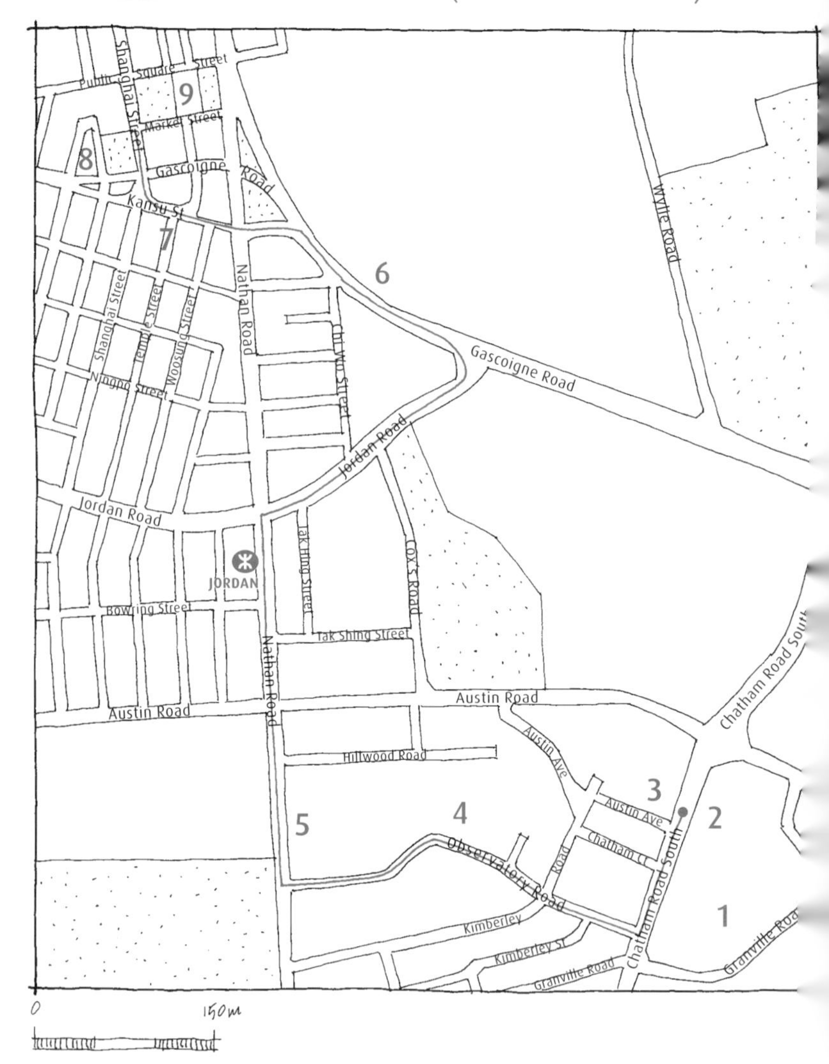

KEY

1. Hong Kong Science Museum
2. Hong Kong Museum of History
3. Rosary Church
4. Observatory
5. St Andrew's Church
6. Old South Kowloon District Court
7. Temple Street Night Market
8. Jade Market
9. Tin Hau Temple

Hong Kong Science Museum

Hong Kong Science Museum ❶

This multi-storey museum houses exhibitions on computers, energy, physics, robotics, telecommunications and health. The area in front of the building is divided into an upper and lower piazza joined by a wide staircase that can double up as seating for outdoor presentations. Among the outdoor exhibits are a large sundial, an echo wall, a pool that responds to sound frequencies, and another pool that uses fibre optics to make coloured patterns in the water. Very much a "hands-on" type of place, this museum is popular with children and draws in the crowds on weekends and holidays.

Hong Kong Science Museum
1–9pm Mon–Wed and Fri; 10am–9pm Sat–Sun and public holidays
Admission charges, but free on Wed
www.hk.science.museum
Tel: 2732 3232

Hong Kong Museum of History ❷

Next to the Science Museum is the Museum of History, which covers 6000 years of Hong Kong's geography and geology, flora and fauna. There is a distinct emphasis on folk culture, especially that of the Hakka and Haklo ethnic groups. The displays showcase aspects of everyday life such as furniture and clothing, and there is even a mock-up of a 19th-century Hong Kong street, complete with a herbal medicine shop. Perhaps the most interesting parts of the collection are the 19th- and early 20th-century photographs that show what daily life used to be like in the city.

Hong Kong Museum of History
10am–6pm Mon and Wed–Sat; 10am–7pm Sun and public holidays
Admission charges, but free on Wed
www.lcsd.gov.hk/ce/Museum/History
Tel: 2724 9042

Rosary Church ❸

Across Chatham Road South from the Hong Kong Museum of History you will find the Rosary Church, a pleasingly symmetrical building in the Gothic style. Built in 1905 to cater to a burgeoning Roman Catholic community in this part of Hong Kong, its construction was enabled thanks to a generous donation from Dr Anthony Gomes, originally from Portugal. To the right sits a Neoclassical school building with elegant arched verandas.

> **Did You Know?**
> While fleeing Mongol invaders, the last Sung Emperor seeing Kowloon for the first time counted eight mountains and decided to call them the "eight dragons". An obsequious courtier suggested that it should perhaps be nine rather than eight since the emperor himself should be considered a dragon. The emperor was delighted and dubbed the place *gau lung* — literally, "nine dragons".

Observatory ❹

Retrace your steps back down Chatham Road South and turn right onto Observatory Road. The Hong Kong Observatory, which doubles as a weather station, will be on your right where the road makes a bend to the left. This is a fairly secluded, spacious area — a pleasant surprise amid the bustle of Kowloon. The Observatory was built in 1884 as part of a chain of observatories operating in Asia from the early 1870s that also included Beijing, Jakarta, Manila and Shanghai. This small hill at the centre of Tsim Sha Tsui was known as Mount Elgin, and was deemed an ideal location because it had good sight-lines in all directions. The hill had actually been reserved for the governor's Kowloon residence, but the need for a weather station took precedence.

St Andrew's Church ❺

Continue along Observatory Road, turn right at Nathan Road, and you will see St Andrew's Church on your right. Designed in early English Gothic style, this pleasant red-brick church was built in 1905. It was a gift from the government and was funded by Sir Paul Chater, an Armenian financier with business interests in Hong Kong. During the Japanese occupation, it was used as a rice store and later a Buddhist temple.

St Andrew's Church

Old South Kowloon District Court ❻

Continue along Nathan Road and turn right onto Jordan Road, then make a left turn at Gascoigne Road and you will see the Old South Kowloon District Court on your right on the other side of the elevated roadway. Sitting imposingly on a hill overlooking Gascoigne Road and approached via twin granite staircases, the courthouse was built in 1934 and is still in use — today as the Lands Tribunal. The handsome granite-and-brick building is fronted by a colonnade of Corinthian columns, but its outlook has unfortunately been spoiled by the elevated stretch of Gascoigne Road running in front of it and blocking its view from the distance.

Temple Street Night Market ❼

Continue along Gascoigne Road and take the left bend where the road forks. Then cross Nathan Road onto Kansu Street. Temple Street will be the second street on your left. The night market, stretching south along Temple Street towards Ning Po Street, used to cater to men's goods such as clothing, as well as cheap watches and electronics. There are still plenty of men's items for sale, but it now also stocks pirated CDs, fake designer goods, footwear, kitchenware and other everyday items. This is one of the more lively markets

Old South Kowloon District Court

in Hong Kong and a good place to bargain. Food stalls offer a wide range of snacks, and there are seafood and hotpot restaurants nearby.

Temple Street Night Market
4pm–midnight daily
Admission free

Jade Market ❽

Located on Kansu Street, near the Gascoigne Road overpass, this market houses hundreds of stalls selling a wide variety of different grades of jade, including rough as well as polished stones, and finished items of jewellery.

Note: Jade
To the Chinese, jade is considered the most precious of stones. Used for decoration and jewellery, it is also believed to have certain magical qualities, including the power to prevent ageing and to deter evil spirits. Though usually green, jade can also be black, red or white. Carvings have symbolic significance: a deer means wealth and luck, a tiger represents blessings from the gods, while a dragon symbolises power and vigour.

It is an interesting market to wander around in, but unless you know what you're doing, or have someone with you who does, you should be wary of making expensive purchases. The best time to visit is in the morning.

Jade Market
9am–6pm daily
Admission free

Note: Bamboo Scaffolding
Local construction workers prefer bamboo scaffolding to steel because it is five times cheaper and four times faster to raise, not to mention significantly lighter. It withstands typhoons better than steel, and moreover gives warning before failing. Scaffolders have their very own god, different from the god of the building trade, but the same one as prayed to by Cantonese opera troupes — whose stages are made of bamboo. They grip the poles with their legs, and don't use safety nets or harnesses. It is no wonder then that "fall-off person" is listed as the number-two cause of work-related deaths in Hong Kong.

Tin Hau Temple ❾

Retrace your steps down Kansu Street and turn left onto Shanghai Street; take a right onto Market Street, and the Tin Hau Temple will be ahead of you on your left, overlooking the square. This temple is dedicated to Tin Hau, the goddess of seafarers. Traditional in its form and layout, the temple complex also houses a shrine to Shing Wong, the city deity, who ensures justice — which is why he is shown surrounded by judges and soldiers.

Tin Hau Temple
8am–5.30pm daily
Admission free

End of Kowloon walks.

Further Afield

Further Afield

This chapter covers individual but isolated places of interest, such as the Law Uk Folk Museum and Stanley Market on Hong Kong Island; the Ten Thousand Buddhas Temple in Sha Tin in the New Territories; and the Tian Tan Buddha Statue at the Po Lin Monastery on Lantau Island.

FURTHER AFIELD: Hong Kong Island

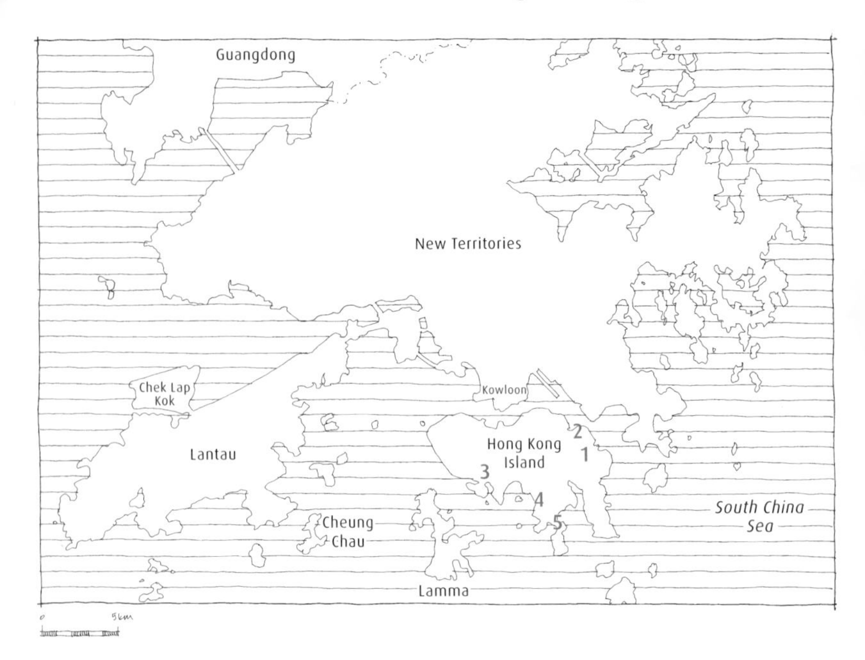

KEY

1. Law Uk Folk Museum
2. Museum of Coastal Defence
3. Aberdeen
4. Repulse Bay
5. Stanley

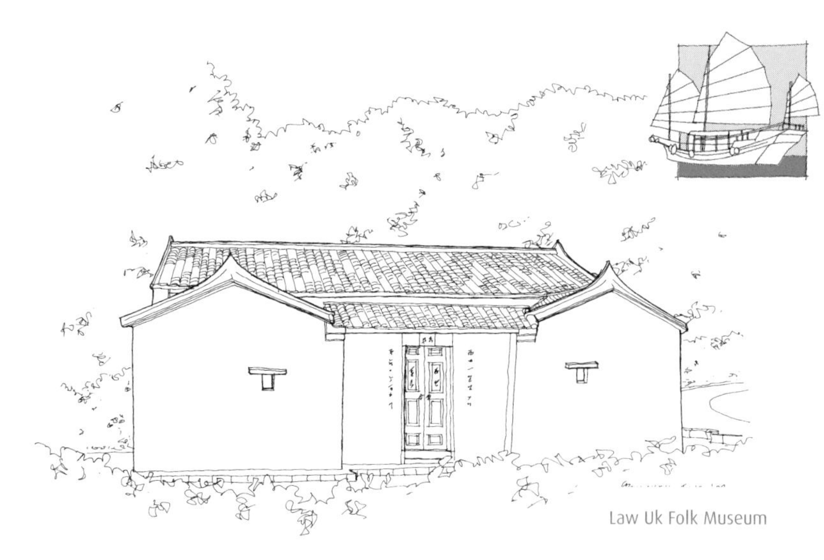
Law Uk Folk Museum

Law Uk Folk Museum  

Located at No. 14 Kut Shing Street in Chai Wan (nearest MTR: Chai Wan — not to be confused with Wan Chai), this is an interesting museum, although a little rundown. It contains a lot of puppetry displays, and the museum itself is a restored Hakka residence with some traditional furniture and household items such as farm tools.

Law Uk Folk Museum
10am–6pm Mon–Wed and Fri–Sat; 1–6pm Sun and public holidays
Admission free
www.lcsd.gov.hk/ce/Museum/History/lawuk
Tel: 2896 7006

Museum of Coastal Defence  

Located in the Shau Kei Wan district, at No. 175 Tung Hei Road (a 15-minute walk from the Shau Kei Wan MTR station), this museum is housed in the old Lei Yue Mun Fort, one of Hong Kong's oldest and best preserved coastal fortresses. It was built in 1887 to defend the eastern approaches of the harbour against attack from Russia and France. It still retains its batteries, underground magazines, protective ditch and torpedo station. The museum itself covers 600 years of Hong Kong's coastal defences, from the Ming and Qing dynasties' efforts against pirates and Western imperialists, through the Opium Wars, to the Territory's role as a major base for the British Navy, the Japanese invasion in 1941, and, finally, the 1997 Handover.

Museum of Coastal Defence
10am–5pm Fri–Wed
Admission charges
www.lcsd.gov.hk/ce/Museum/Coastal
Tel: 2569 1500

Aberdeen ❸

Take Bus No. 7, 70, 91 or 94 from Exchange Square in Central to get to Aberdeen, a pretty little harbour town named after Lord Aberdeen, Britain's Foreign Secretary in the 1840s. Known in Chinese as Heung Gong Tsai (Little Fragrant Harbour), it is one of the oldest settlements in Hong Kong and thought to have been the origin of the whole Territory's name. It is home to a small community of fishermen who live on their boats, though most descendants of the original Tanka and Haklo boat-people now live in the surrounding high-rise buildings. The string of floating restaurants specialising in seafood is a big attraction. There is also a small **Tin Hau Temple**, built in 1851, which is made up of several courtyards linked via traditional "moon gates"— circular portals in the garden walls.

Repulse Bay ❹

Take Bus No. 6, 66 or 260 from Exchange Square in Central to get to Repulse Bay. The bus ride itself is quite spectacular, with dramatic views as you descend towards the coast. Named for a 19th-century British warship, Repulse Bay has an excellent beach — which can get very crowded in the summer — and is home to some of the most expensive real estate in Hong Kong. Of particular interest is **Repulse Bay Apartments**, formerly Repulse Bay Hotel (built 1922), in its day a stylish haunt for locals and international travellers. Sipping afternoon tea on its airy verandas overlooking the bay was a fashionable pastime for the colonial elite. The hotel was demolished in 1982, but the apartments which replaced it have tried to recapture some of the glamour of the hotel's heyday.

Stanley ❺

Take Bus No. 6, 66 or 260 from Exchange Square in Central to get to the seaside town of Stanley. The buses pass through Repulse Bay, and it is just another five minutes to get here. Named after Lord Stanley — the British Secretary of State for War and the Colonies in the 1840s and thrice Prime Minister — it was one of the island's largest settlements at the time, with about 2000 inhabitants when the British took over in 1841. The main attraction of the town, apart from the local restaurants, which are generally quite good, is **Stanley Market**. It is not perhaps the best value in Hong Kong, and you will find fairly ordinary fare such as jewellery, shoes, clothes and Chinese souvenirs, but the market itself is housed in an elaborate maze of alleyways, and this is what makes it interesting.

Now home to a restaurant, **88 Stanley Village Road** was originally built in 1859 as a police station, and is one of a select number of buildings protected under the Antiquities and Monuments Ordinance.

The **Murray Building** was originally built as an officers' mess in Central in 1843 and is said to have been used as a torture chamber by the Japanese during the occupation. Despite being listed as a Grade I Monument, it was demolished to make way for the Bank of China Tower, whereupon it was moved stone by stone and re-erected in 1998 as an upmarket shopping and restaurant complex. The massive stone structure dominates the bay.

St Stephen's Beach is a popular recreation spot, while the **Stanley Military Cemetery** is a serene and beautiful place. Some of its graves date back as far as 1843. It was reopened for use from 1942 for a few years to bury those who died at the hands of the Japanese.

Stanley Market
10am–6pm daily
Admission free

Murray Building, Stanley

FURTHER AFIELD: New Territories

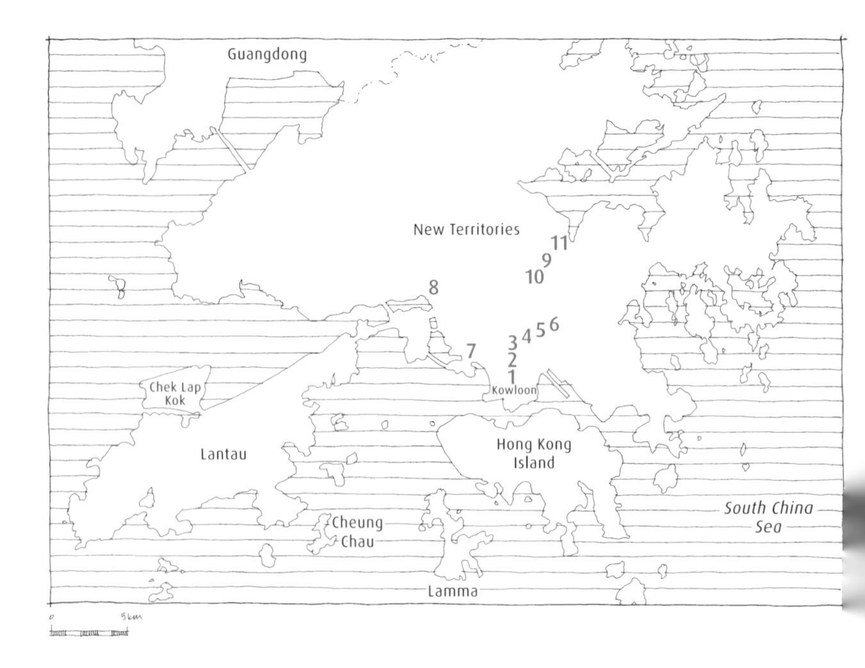

KEY

1. Mong Kok
2. Ladies' Market
3. Flower Market
4. Yuen Po Street Bird Garden
5. Kowloon Walled City Park
6. Chi Lin Nunnery
7. Lei Cheng Uk Han Tomb
8. Sam Tung Uk Museum
9. Ten Thousand Buddhas Temple
10. Heritage Museum
11. Sha Tin Racecourse

New Territories

The New Territories are largely rural; in fact more than 70 per cent of Hong Kong's total area is still listed as being for rural use or protected as country parkland. Most parts of the New Territories are crossed with trails that connect villages along the few roads encircling the mountains. These roads cut through uninhabited hills, abandoned rice fields and secluded inlets that show a quieter, greener side to Hong Kong.

Mong Kok ❶

Nearest MTR: Mong Kok. This area north of Tsim Sha Tsui on the Kowloon Peninsula is where the locals go to shop and is particularly good for clothing bargains. While the stalls are rather basic and the selection limited, the prices are half those in other parts of the city.

Ladies' Market ❷

Nearest MTR: Mong Kok. The Ladies' Market on Tung Choi Street starts at noon, but the best time to visit is between 6pm and 10pm. It sells cheap clothing and even cheaper jewellery in a bustling market atmosphere.

Ladies' Market
Noon–10.30pm daily
Admission free

Flower Market

Flower Market ❸

A 10-minute walk north of Ladies' Market, just beyond Prince Edward Road West, is a wonderful flower market — actually a long row of flower shops spreading their wares out onto the pavement and street all along one side of the appropriately named Flower Market Street.

Flower Market
7am–7pm daily
Admission free

Yuen Po Street Bird Garden ❹

Walk along Flower Market Street, past Mong Kok Stadium, and you will come to the Yuen Po Street Bird Garden. This is home to hundreds of bird-sellers who keep their chirpy wares in elaborate teak and bamboo cages. The Chinese have always kept songbirds as pets and looked after them lovingly — some birds are fed with chopsticks and given honey to improve their vocal cords. Elderly Hong Kongers can be seen watching the birds for hours on end.

Yuen Po Street Bird Garden
7am–7pm daily
Admission free

Yuen Po Street Bird Garden

> **Note: Mahjong**
> Call *ma jeuk* by the Cantonese, the game was introduced to the West as mahjong by an American called Babcock in the 1920s. It is played everywhere in Hong Kong, and in the evening you will be able to hear the distinctive clatter of the tiles being "washed" (shuffled on the table in preparation for a new game) through many an open window. Players try to make sets and sequences, much in the vein of rummy.

Kowloon Walled City Park

Kowloon Walled City Park ❺

Nearest MTR: Lok Fu. This is all that is left of what used to be one of the most remarkable places in the city: the Kowloon Walled City, an enclave that was under Chinese jurisdiction despite being at the heart of a British colony. Not being subject to British law, it developed organically into an unregulated, riotous labyrinth, with buildings up to a dozen storeys high pressing up against one another, leaving the narrowest of alleyways between them that rarely saw the sun. With more than 30,000 people crammed into this small plot of 6.5 acres, it was one of the most densely inhabited places in the world. The British knocked it down shortly before their rule ended, and it has now been converted into this little park. The old *yamen*, or administrative building, has been kept and shows photos and information about the history of this fascinating but now vanished place.

Kowloon Walled City Park
6.30am–11pm daily
Exhibition: 10am–6pm Thurs–Tue
Admission free

Chi Lin Nunnery ❻

Nearest MTR: Diamond Hill. Located at No. 5 Chi Lin Drive is the largest Buddhist nunnery in East Asia. Its layout and architectural expression follow the traditional Chinese style and make for a serene respite from the concrete and chaos of the rest of the city. There are a number of pavilions and halls arranged around lotus ponds, all symmetrically aligned along the nunnery's central axis. The Hall of Celestial Kings contains a statue of the Maitreya Buddha, also known as the Buddha of the Future. The most impressive statue in the whole complex is the golden Sakyamuni Buddha, which sits on a lotus altar in the Main Hall.

The nunnery sits on a gently sloping hill that overlooks the **Nan Lian Garden**. This has to be one of the most delightful traditional Chinese gardens in the city. Laid out according to the principles of Tang dynasty garden design, paths wind their way gently through meticulously manicured shrubs and trees to reveal glimpses of pools and pavilions all artfully arranged in the Chinese style.

Chi Lin Nunnery
9am–4.30pm daily
Admission free

Nan Lian Garden
7am–9pm daily
Admission free

Nan Lian Garden

Lei Cheng Uk Han Tomb ❼

Nearest MTR: Cheung Sha Wan Station. At No. 41 Tonkin Street sits this 2000-year-old cross-shaped burial vault. Constructed during the late Han dynasty, this tomb was discovered in 1955 when the hillside was being levelled to make way for the Lei Cheng Uk housing estate. Fifty-eight funerary objects were found inside — mostly everyday items intended to accompany the dead beyond the grave. However, no skeletal remains were unearthed. The tomb itself is now encased in concrete and can only be glimpsed through a window, while the artefacts are on display in the on-site museum.

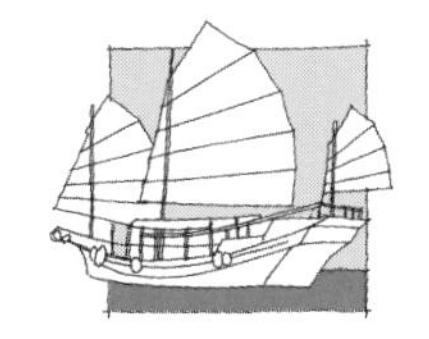

Lei Cheng Uk Han Tomb
10am–6pm Mon–Wed and Fri–Sat; 1–6pm Sun
Admission free
Tel: 2386 2863

Sam Tung Uk Museum ❽

Nearest MTR: Tsuen Wan. Located at No. 2 Kwu Uk Lane, the clean, simple lines of this 17th-century Hakka dwelling disguise the richness of the ornate interior of the central ancestral hall. Now surrounded by high-rise housing, this was actually built as a small walled village to protect the Chan clan from the pirates that plagued this part of the coast. Its name means "three-beam dwelling" because of the three central beams (*tung*) supporting the roofs over the building's three halls.

Sam Tung Uk Museum
9am–5pm Wed–Mon
Admission free
Tel: 2411 2001

Sam Tung Uk Museum

Ten Thousand Buddhas Temple

Ten Thousand Buddhas Temple ⑨  

Follow the signs from Sha Tin MTR Station. The monastery, better known as the Ten Thousand Buddhas Temple, was founded in 1957 by the monk, Yuet Kai. After he died in 1965 at the age of 87 — it is said he predicted the date of his death — his body did not decompose. His corpse, now covered in gold leaf, is on display here. The entire complex is home to an estimated 13,000 Buddha statues, all of which were donated by the faithful. The courtyard has a lovely view over Sha Tin and the surrounding countryside.

Ten Thousand Buddhas Temple
9am–5pm daily
Admission free
www.10kbuddhas.org

Heritage Museum ⑩

This museum, located in a pseudo-traditional Chinese building at No. 1 Man Lam Road in Sha Tin, was opened in 2000 and has on display a bit of everything, from Cantonese opera to comics. There is also a children's toy gallery as well as an art gallery containing the impressive collection of Dr T.T. Tsui.

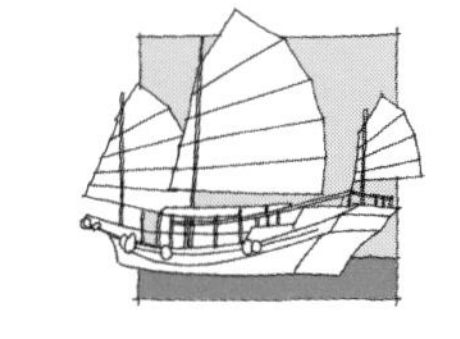

Heritage Museum
10am–6pm Mon and Wed–Sat; 10am–7pm Sun
Admission charges, but free on Wed
www.heritagemuseum.gov.hk
Tel: 2180 8188

Sha Tin Racecourse ⓫

Horse racing is a Hong Kong obsession. Races are held on Wednesday nights, Saturday afternoons and sometimes on Sunday from September to June at both of Hong Kong's racecourses. Visitors staying in Hong Kong less than 21 days can attend the races on special terms courtesy of the Hong Kong Jockey Club.

Sha Tin Racecourse
Call for race times
Admission charges
www.sha-tin.com
Tel: 2696 3210

FURTHER AFIELD: Outlying Islands

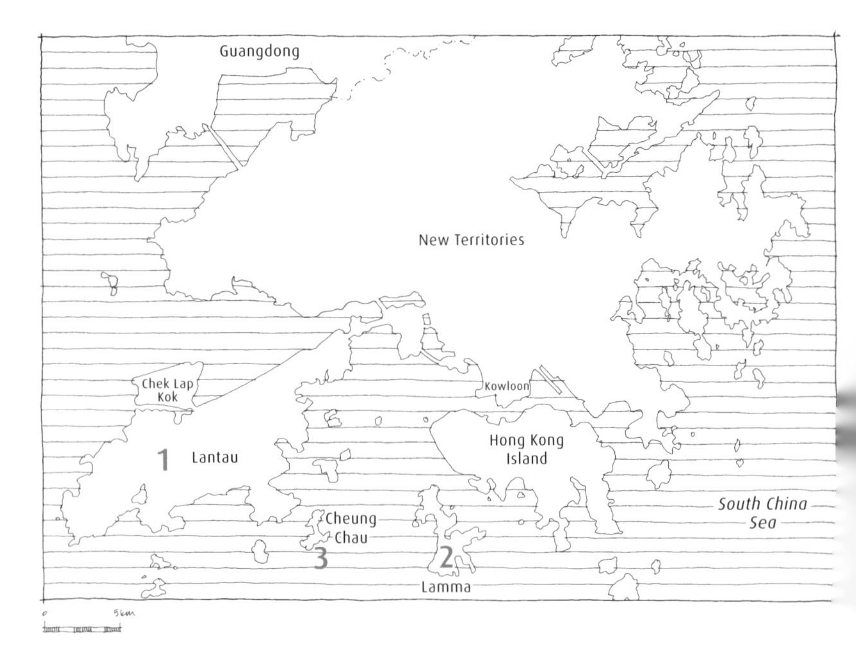

KEY

1. Lantau
2. Lamma
3. Cheung Chau

Outlying Islands

Hong Kong's outlying islands are charming, each having its individual character, which makes them well worth taking the time to explore — from majestic Lantau island, with its huge Tian Tan Buddha Statue, to smaller Lamma, which is good for hiking. Tiny Cheung Chau is a quaint fishing village that hosts a bizarre annual Bun Festival.

Lantau ❶

Lantau is large — almost twice the size of Hong Kong Island — but sparsely populated. More than half of this mountainous island has been declared country parks, with good hiking routes, and there are a number of interesting places to visit, such as the fishing village of Tai O, Tung Chung Fort and a tea farm (established in 1959 by a Briton and the only tea plantation in Hong Kong), as well as some charming monasteries like the Ying Ming Monastery and the Po Lin Monastery. Lantau is also home to Hong Kong International Airport (Chek Lap Kok) and the impressive Tsing Ma Bridge, which links it to the rest of the Territory.

Lantau
Location: 20–30 km west of Central
Train: MTR Airport Railway Link to Tung Chung, then take a taxi
Ferry: Central/Tsim Sha Tsui to Mui Wo on Lantau, then Bus No. 2 to Po Lin
www.afdparks.gov.hk

Ngong Ping 360 Cable Car

With its glass-floored gondolas, the cable car is a spectacular way to see the island of Lantau. It starts a short walk from Tung Chung MTR station and travels to Ngong Ping, where it is possible to go to the Po Lin Monastery and the Tian Tan Buddha Statue.

Ngong Ping 360 Cable Car
10am–6pm Mon–Fri; 9am–6.30pm Sat–Sun
Admission charges

Tian Tan Buddha Statue

Po Lin Monastery, situated high on a plateau and built in the style of a traditional Chinese Buddhist temple, is charming to visit, if a little noisy, and its restaurant serves excellent vegetarian meals. Its main claim to fame, however, is the huge **Tian Tan Buddha Statue**, reputed to be the tallest bronze sculpture in the world. Made in Nanjing by the satellite and

Tian Tan Buddha Statue

rocket manufacturers China Astronomical Industry Scientific and Consultative Corporation, it was assembled in Hong Kong and is roughly the height of a 10-storey building. The views from the statue's podium, up a long flight of stairs, are worth the climb.

Po Lin Monastery
10am–6pm daily
Admission free
www.plm.org.hk
Tel: 2985 5248

Lamma ❷

The third-largest island in the Territory, after Lantau and Hong Kong, Lamma is famous for its seafood restaurants, beaches and hiking trails. The walk between the two main villages, Yung Shue Wan and Sok Kwu Wan, both of which have ferry access, takes about 90 minutes and passes by the popular Hung Shing Ye Beach. South of the beach, a small path climbs steeply to a pavilion, a pleasant place to relax — if you can ignore the power station. Nearby is a ridge where you can look down on the village of Sok Kwu Wan, where there are a number of good seafood restaurants by the waterfront.

Lamma
Location: 10 km south of Central
Ferry: Central/Aberdeen to Yung Shue Wan/Sok Kwu Wan piers

Cheung Chau ❸

Cheung Chau is about 4 km from end to end and used to be called Dumbbell Island because of its distinctive shape. It is known for its seafood restaurants on Praya Street and its traditional shops selling paper offerings, herbs and incense on San Hing Street. The beach at the end of Tung Wan Road is also a popular destination. Cars are not allowed on the island, so most people get around on foot, bicycle or boat. You can still see the traditional **houseboats** of the Haklo people in the harbour. Other interesting places to visit include the Cheung Po-tsai Cave (an old pirate hang-out), the Kwan Kung Pavilion (dedicated to Kwan Tai, the God of War and Righteousness), and the Pak Tai Temple, home of the famous Bun Festival.

Cheung Chau
Location: 20 km southwest of Central
Ferry: Central/Lantau to Sai Wan

> **Note: Bun Festival**
> This festival takes place in front of the Pak Tai Temple on the island of Cheung Chau every year in May. It is famous for its "bun towers", consisting of bamboo frames, often up to 20 metres high, covered with thousands of pink-and-white lotus-paste buns. The festival came about after the discovery of human bones during construction work on the temple; this led the islanders to make offerings of steamed buns to appease any spirits angered by the disturbance. The highlight of the festival is the procession in which children are dressed as gods and are carried above the crowd.

Haklo boat-people

Macau

Approximate walking time: 4 hours

MACAU

It would be a pity to be in Hong Kong and not visit Macau. Even if an overnight stay is not possible, the territory is so small that it is possible to see most of the city centre's main sights in a day. Only 65 km from Hong Kong but about 300 years older, it is a fascinating mix of Portuguese and Chinese culture.

Macau Peninsula

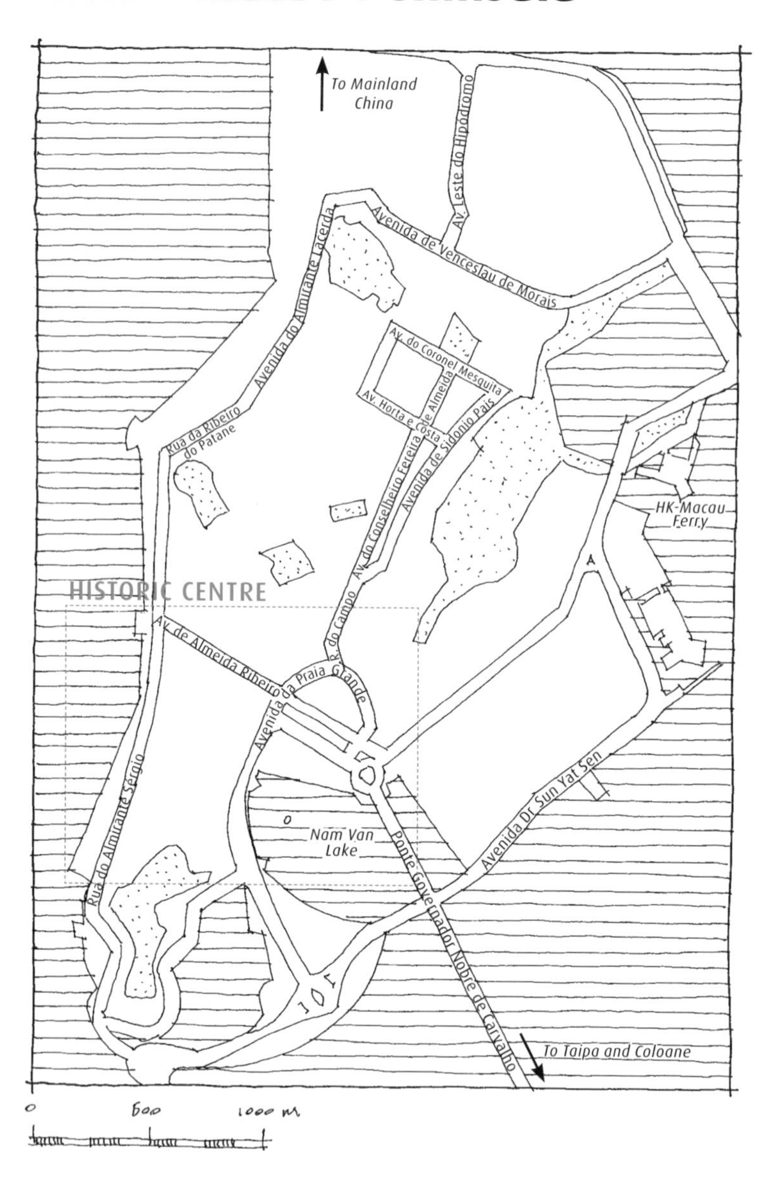

Introduction

History

When the Portuguese settled in Macau in 1557, they were in an ideal position to trade. Firstly, the Chinese were not allowed to leave their country under penalty of death. Secondly, the Japanese, after having attempted an invasion once too often, were banned from the country. And lastly, the existing trade was almost exclusively in the hands of Muslims, whom the Portuguese were eager to supplant as middlemen, believing that a blow against the Muslims would be a victory for the Roman Catholic faith. Macau became a centre for Christianity in the Far East and flourished as an outpost for all the other European countries trading with China, a position it held until the British set up their colony of Hong Kong in 1841.

Thereafter the importance of Macau was eclipsed, although it continued to be an important distribution centre for goods such as rice and fish. It remained under Portuguese rule until 20 December 1999 and is now a Special Administrative Region of China.

Owing to land reclamation, the Macau that was handed back to China was about twice the size of the territory the Portuguese first settled — though still tiny, at just 30 sq km. It is divided into the Macau Peninsula and two islands, called Taipa and Coloane, all connected by bridges. About 95 per cent of the population is Chinese. Gambling has been legal in Macau for more than 150 years, and most tourists are Chinese gamblers drawn to the casinos.

Language

The official language is Portuguese, but English is widely spoken, and is the language of trade, commerce and tourism. Most locals, however, speak Cantonese.

Climate

The climate is similar to Hong Kong's (see page 8), but with cooler sea breezes during the summer.

Getting There

Macau has an international airport, but most visitors arrive via Hong Kong, in which case a ferry transfer — approximately 1 hour — makes the most sense. There are two terminals with services to Macau: one on Hong Kong Island, at Shun Tak Centre in the Central district; and one in Kowloon, at China Hong Kong City in Tsim Sha Tsui (see page 134).

MACAU: HISTORIC CENTRE

KEY

1. Maritime Museum
2. A-Ma Temple
3. Colina da Penha
4. São Lourenco
5. Dom Pedro V Theatre
6. Santo Agostinho
7. Leal Senado
8. Largo Senado
9. São Francisco Barracks
10. Macau Cathedral (Sé)
11. Santa Casa da Misericordia
12. São Domingo
13. São Paulo (ruins)
14. Monte Fort and Museum

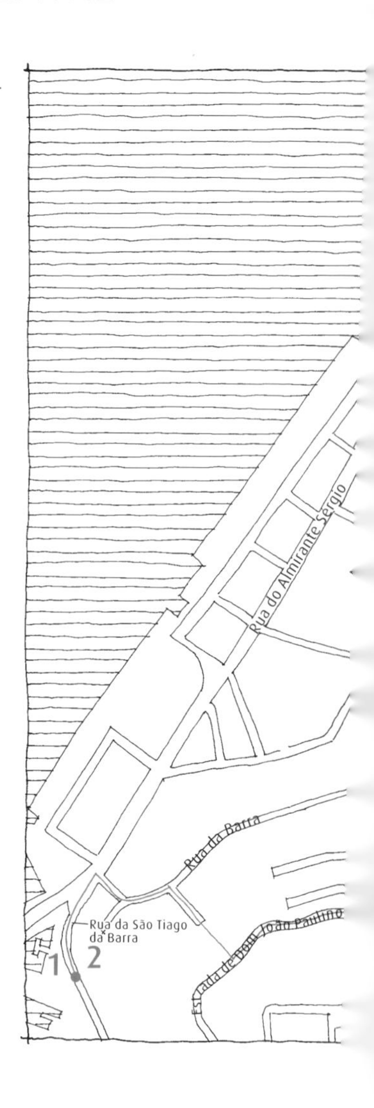

Rua de São Paulo
7 13 14
12
R. de São Domingo
Avenida de Almeida Ribeiro
11
10
8
7
Rua do Campo
9
Calçada do Gamboa
Calçada do Tronco Velho
6
Avenida da Praia Grande
Rua Central
5
Calçada de S. Agostinho
Avenida do Infante Dom Henrique
Travessa do Paiva
4
Travessa do Padre Narciso
António
Avenida da Praia Grande
Nam Van Lake
200m
100
0

Maritime Museum ❶

Located on Rua de São Tiago da Barra, this small but interesting museum is best reached by taxi. Home to exhibits that explain the history of shipping in this part of Asia, particularly the South China Sea, with its fascinating but deadly pirates, this is an ideal place to start walking through the oldest and longest-lasting European colony in East Asia.

Maritime Museum
10am–5.30pm Wed–Mon
Admission charges, but free on Sun

A-Ma Temple ❷

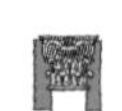

Across the road from the Maritime Museum is the A-Ma Temple. Nestling at the foot of Colina da Penha, it is the oldest Chinese place of worship in the city. Dating back 6000 years, it was here when Portugal was ceded the territory in 1557. Originally believed to have been built by local fishermen, it was dedicated to their patron goddess, Tin Hau, known locally as A-Ma.

A-Ma Temple
10am–6pm daily
Admission free

Colina da Penha ❸

Climb Colina da Penha and you will be able to enjoy panoramic views. The **Chapel of Our Lady of Penha** has been standing here since 1622 but its current incarnation largely dates from 1837. You can follow the heritage signs marking the UNESCO World Heritage route to see an old **Bishop's Palace** and the **Largo do Lilau**, a pretty little plaza and one of the oldest Portuguese places of residence in the city. Nearby is the **Casa da Mandarin** (Mandarin's House), a traditional Chinese courtyard house built in 1881, while the nearby **Moorish Barracks** was built in 1874 to house policemen who had come here from the Portuguese enclave of Goa in India.

Moorish Barracks
9am–6pm daily
Admission free

São Lourenco ❹

Leave Colina da Penha and follow Rua do Padre Antonio and you will come to the church of São Lourenco on your left. This magnificent symmetrical church sits atop an imposing double staircase. Its pretty yellow-and-white

Governor's House

facade contrasts dramatically with the lush greenery of its garden. Dedicated to St Lawrence, it was first built in the 1560s and largely rebuilt in the 1840s.

Follow the narrow street from the front of São Lourenco and you will come out onto Avenida da Praia Grande. The **Governor's House** will be on your left overlooking the avenue. This is an elegant stone mansion, painted a deep pink, the stone detailing of its windows and balconies in a very fine Neoclassical style. The gardens are beautifully maintained and feature formal paths, clipped hedges and lotus ponds.

The **Avenida da Praia Grande** was originally the seafront and a fashionable place to promenade. Home to some handsome old buildings (many with arcades) and some less-successful modern ones, the curving street still makes for a pleasant walk.

São Lourenco
10am–4pm Mon–Fri;
10am–1pm Sat
Admission free

Pagoda, Avenida da Praia Grande

Dom Pedro V Theatre

Dom Pedro V Theatre ❺

Continue along the Avenida da Praia Grande until you have passed the end of the lake on your right and take the next left. The **Dom Pedro V Theatre** will be ahead of you at the top of this steep street. Built in 1860 as the first Western-style theatre in China, it is still doing business as a place for concerts and plays, particularly during Macau's numerous arts festivals. An elegantly symmetrical Neoclassical building, it is graced by a spacious portico and some rather fine plasterwork decoration.

Continue uphill past the theatre and you will come to a small plaza, Largo de Santo Agostinho, which is overlooked by **St Joseph's Seminary**. The entrance is around the corner on Rua do Seminario. This was set up in 1728 as a Jesuit mission in China. Now its classrooms and lecture halls are empty but its chapel is particularly attractive and well worth a visit. The statues in it were salvaged from the ruins of São Paulo.

St Joseph's Seminary Chapel
10am–5pm daily
Admission free

Santo Agostinho ❻

On the other side of Largo de Santo Agostinho from the Seminary sits the church that gives the square its name. Santo Agostinho is a lovely Baroque place of worship, and the largest in its style in the region. Founded in 1586

by a Spanish order of Augustinians, it was rebuilt in 1814, but its elaborate facade was only completed around 1875.

Across the narrow street leading out from the square is the **Sir Robert Ho Tung Library**, another fine building in the Portuguese colonial style.

Sir Robert Ho Tung Library
10am–7pm Mon–Sat; 11am–7pm Sun
Admission free

Leal Senado 7

Continue down the narrow street and you will come to Avenida de Almeida Ribeiro. The Leal Senado will be on your right overlooking this wide thoroughfare. Its name means "loyal senate" in English, and comes from the fact that its members refused to recognise Spanish sovereignty over Portugal during the 60-year occupation of the country in the 17th century. Regarded as one of the best examples of traditional Portuguese architecture in the city, it overlooks one of the most important junctions in the city: where Avenida de Almeida Ribeiro meets the Largo Senado, Macau's main civic square. The Leal Senado wielded huge power in the early days of Macau, but now is home to a considerably less powerful Municipal Council. The building was recently restored and now also houses a public library.

Facing the Leal Senado across Avenida de Almeida Ribeiro is the imposing **General Post Office**. A fine Neoclassical building which turns the corner from Avenida de Almeida Ribeiro onto Largo Senado very well, it has a nicely detailed clock tower.

Leal Senado
9am–9pm daily
Admission free

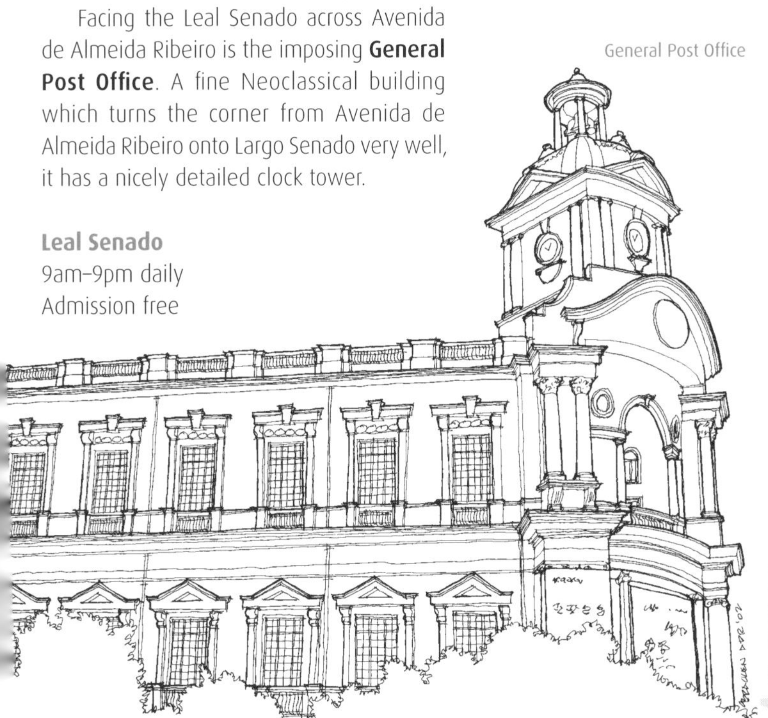

General Post Office

Largo Senado 8

The Leal Senado overlooks the Largo Senado (Senate Square), one of the most important as well as the most picturesque public places in the city. Surrounded by some of the city's finest buildings, including the General Post Office and the church of São Domingo, its irregular shape leads onto Rua da Palha, a shopping district full of narrow winding streets and laneways, paved in an eye-catching black-and-white wave pattern.

São Francisco Barracks 9

Return to the Avenida de Almeida Ribeiro, turn left, and you will be back out on the Avenida da Praia Grande. Continue along the avenue as it sweeps around to the right and you will see the São Francisco Barracks ahead of you on the other side of Rua do Campo. This elegant barracks is home to a military museum as well as a military club. The long, L-shaped building was built in a simple Neoclassical style and has been painted with warm Mediterranean colours. The gardens consist of well-pruned flower beds and wide paths leading down to a handsome stone staircase. The upper level, with its round tower built to honour World War I veterans, has been converted into the headquarters of the Association for the Handicapped.

São Francisco Barracks

São Francisco Barracks
9am–5.45pm Mon–Fri;
9am–5pm Sat–Sun
Admission free

Macau Cathedral (Sé) 10

Retrace your steps back along the Avenida da Praia Grande and take the first right, a steep, narrow little street at the top of which is a small square overlooked by Macau Cathedral, also known as the Sé. This is the principal church of the Roman Catholic Diocese of Macau, which used to include all of China, Japan and Korea. A somewhat sombre building, particularly when compared to some of the other more colourful places of worship in the city, it is nonetheless a very fine example of the Neoclassical style and also contains some lovely stained-glass windows.

Santa Casa da Misericordia 11

Cross the little square and follow the narrow street downhill until you come out onto Largo Senado again. The white Neoclassical-style building facing the fountain is Santa Casa da Misericordia. Its name in English means the "Holy House of Mercy", and it is a small museum dedicated to religious paraphernalia.

Santa Casa da Misericordia
10am–1pm and 2.30–5.30pm, Mon–Sat
Admission charges

São Domingo 12

At the north end of the Largo Senado is the church of São Domingo. This is regarded as one of the most beautiful of Macau's Baroque churches, as well as one of the oldest. Built in the 17th century by a Spanish order of Dominicans, it is painted a pleasant light yellow and houses an impressive tiered altar with images of the Virgin and Child and Our Lady of Fatima. This latter is carried in a procession through the city during the Fatima festival each year in May. There is a small **Museum of Sacred Art** behind the church, full of religious objects and paintings on sacred themes.

Museum of Sacred Art
10am–6pm daily
Admission free

São Domingo

São Paulo (ruins)

São Paulo (ruins) ⓭

Continue past São Domingo and you will come to a busy shopping street. Follow it and you will arrive at what is undoubtedly Macau's most famous sight: the imposing ruined facade of São Paulo. Located at the top of a magnificent flight of stone steps, the impressive facade was built by Christian Japanese artisans who had fled persecution in Nagasaki. It was described as the greatest monument to Christianity in the East when it was completed in the 1620s. The Church of the Mother of God, as São Paulo was officially

named, was built adjoining the Jesuit college of the same name, which was the first Western college in the Far East. A cornerstone dates its construction to 1602. The facade consists of four colonnaded tiers covered with statues and carvings that illustrate the early days of Catholicism in Asia. A Chinese dragon, a single Japanese chrysanthemum, a Portuguese sailing ship, and some pious exhortations in Chinese can be seen as well. After the Jesuits were expelled, the college was used as an army barracks. In 1853, a fire started in the kitchens and destroyed the college and most of the church, leaving only the facade, the mosaic floor and the crypt. An attempt to rebuild it was started in 1904 but seems to have petered out, perhaps just as well, the ruins are so much more remarkable.

São Paulo (ruins)
Open 24 hours
Admission free

Monte Fort and Museum ⑭

This fort sits on the hill to the right of the steps in front of São Paulo. It is in good condition, with cannons in place on the ramparts. It also has wonderful views of the city but is closed between dusk and dawn. It was built by the Jesuits at around the same time as the church, and was the central point of the old city wall that stretched from the village of Patane in the west to the São Francisco Fort on the northern headland of the Bay of Praia Grande. The main event in the fort's history occurred in 1622 when the Dutch were attempting to invade Macau. On 24 June, the feast day of St John the Baptist, a cannonball from the fort's guns landed on a Dutch magazine ship, causing a huge explosion that eventually sank it and destroyed most of the fleet surrounding it. St John the Baptist was immediately hailed as the patron saint of the city. Today, the fort contains the Weather Observatory and the **Museum of Macau**.

Monte Fort
7am–7pm daily
Admission free

Museum of Macau
10am–6pm Tue–Sun
Admission charges, but free on the 15th of the month
www.macaumuseum.gov.mo
Tel: (853) 357 911

End of Macau Historic Centre walk.

MACAU: FURTHER AFIELD

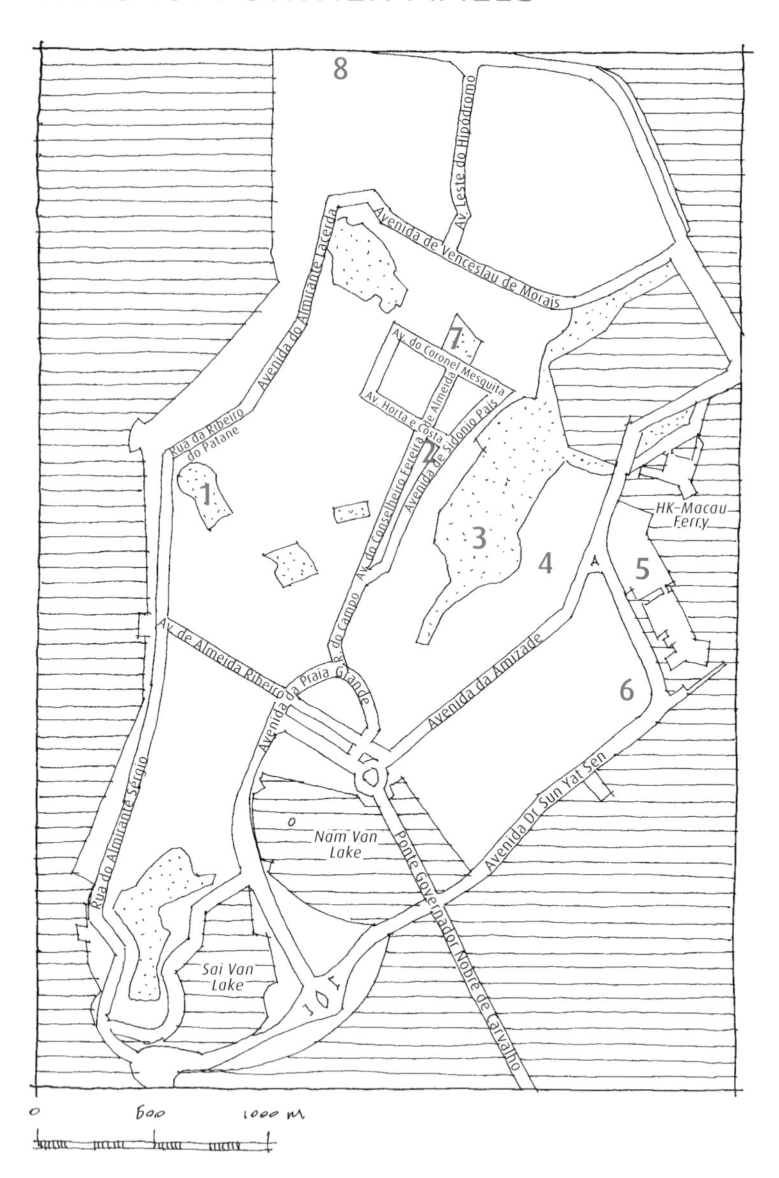

KEY

1. Camões Garden
2. Sun Yat-sen Memorial House
3. Guia Fort and Lighthouse
4. Grand Prix Museum
5. Fisherman's Wharf
6. Macau Museum of Art
7. Kun Iam Temple
8. Portas do Cerco

Camões Garden ❶

Located at the end of Rua de São Paulo (which runs from the back of the São Paulo ruins) is a quiet park named for the famous Portuguese soldier and poet Luis de Camões. Camões is most famous for having written the national Portuguese epic, *The Lusiads*; a bronze bust of him is found in the garden's **Grotto**. Above the Grotto is a small observatory built by the Comte de Lapérouse, a French aristocrat and explorer. The garden was a favourite of George Chinnery, an English artist who spent most of his life on the China coast and painted many lovely scenes of it, and who is buried in the adjoining **Protestant Cemetery**. The cemetery is part of **Casa Garden**, which also features an 18th-century house that was originally home to East India Company officials and is now a cultural institute.

Camões Garden
6am–10pm daily
Admission free

Sun Yat-sen Memorial House

Sun Yat-sen Memorial House 

Located on Avenida de Sidonio Pais near Avenida de Horta e Costa is the Sun Yat-sen House, a memorial (one of many dotted throughout East and Southeast Asia) to the man who became the first president of the Chinese Republic after the overthrow of the Qing dynasty in 1911. Sun studied medicine in Hong Kong and practised in Macau for a number of years. This symmetrical two-storey house, built by Dr Sun's family in an amazingly elaborate Moorish style, replaces the original that blew up when it was being used as an explosives store. It now contains a collection of flags, photographs and other memorabilia.

Located behind it, on Avenida do Conselheiro Ferreira de Almeida, is **Lou Lim Ieoc Garden**, a classical Suzhou-style landscaped garden full of winding paths, pretty little bridges and lotus pools. In the garden's south corner, the Tea Cultural Museum showcases Macau's history as the preeminent entrepot for the tea trade between China and the West.

Sun Yat-sen Memorial House
10am–5pm Wed–Mon
Admission free

Lou Lim Ieoc Garden
6am–9pm daily
Tea Cultural Museum: 9am–7pm Tue–Sun
Admission free

Guia Fort and Lighthouse ❸

Leaving Sun Yat-sen Memorial House, follow Avenida de Sidonio Pais until you come to Calçada do Gaio. Make a left onto this street and the Guia Fortress will be straight ahead of you. The Fortress of Our Lady of Guia — which means "guide" in Portuguese — was built on this 90-metre hill in 1637–38 to defend the border with China. Because it overlooked the entire city, it also became an observation post. The fort's masonry walls rise to a height of about three metres, and two of the original turrets remain. It also contains a barracks, a water cistern, ammunition and equipment stores, the commander's house and a 17th-century chapel dedicated to Our Lady of Guia. A 91m-tall lighthouse, added in 1865, is now the oldest surviving lighthouse on the Chinese coast.

Entrance to lighthouse, Guia Fort

Guia Fort and Lighthouse
9am–5pm daily
Admission free

Grand Prix Museum ❹

Located at No. 431 Rua de Luis Gonzaga Gomes, the Grand Prix Museum tells the story of the world-famous Macau Grand Prix. Formula Three is for cars while there is also a motorcycle Grand Prix, both of which take place each November. Next door is a **Wine Museum**, dedicated to the history of Portuguese wine-making.

Grand Prix Museum
10am–6pm Wed–Mon
Admission charges

Wine Museum
10am–6pm Wed–Mon
Admission charges

Fisherman's Wharf ❺

Close to the Hong Kong Ferry Terminal is Fisherman's Wharf, a theme park with an odd mix of architectural styles — everything from Imperial China to Cape Town and Miami. There's even a volcano, with a rollercoaster inside. Opened in 2006, the complex houses shops and restaurants, boutique hotels, concert venues, amusement rides, and — this being Macau — a casino, naturally.

Fisherman's Wharf
Open 24 hours; rides operate 10am–9pm
Admission free, but charges on rides

Macau Museum of Art ❻

On the opposite side of Fisherman's Wharf from the Hong Kong Ferry Terminal, on Avenida Dr Sun Yat-sen sits the Macau Museum of Art. It houses over five floors an impressive permanent collection of ceramics, calligraphy and art. Next door to the museum is the **Macau Cultural Centre**, which hosts a variety of changing performances in its two auditoria.

Macau Museum of Art
10am–6.30pm Tue–Sun
Admission charges; free on Sundays and public holidays

Kun Iam Temple ❼

Located on Avenida do Coronel Mesquita, near the junction of Rua de Francisco Xavier Pereira and at the foot of Mong Ha Fortress Hill, is the Kun Iam Temple. Dating from 1627, this temple is dedicated to the Goddess of Mercy, and was where the first treaty between China and America was signed, back in 1844. The **Mong Ha Fortress** was built to protect the northern gateway into the colony of Macau. It was constructed in 1849 and is now home to Macau's Institute for Tourism Studies.

Portas do Cerco ❽

A landscaped park now surrounds the gates that once guarded the northern entrance to the Portuguese colony of Macau. Built in 1870, these gates are inscribed with a quote from Portugal's national poet, Luis de Camões: "Honour your country, for your country is watching you"—a fitting admonition for such a place of vigilance.

End of Macau walks.

Architectural Styles

Architectural Styles

This chapter describes some of the architectural styles mentioned in the book, such as Neoclassicism and the Gothic. It also explains traditional Asian building typologies, such as Chinese and Indian temples, mosques, and a special type of building that has all but disappeared from the built environment of Hong Kong: the shophouse.

Pao Kong Temple, Rua da Figueira, Macau

Chinese Temple

The architecture of a Chinese temple is usually based on the traditional Chinese courtyard house, with pavilions built in accordance with the precepts of *feng shui* around open courtyards. A pair of stone lions placed near the entrance serve as notional guards against evil spirits, as do the "door gods" painted on the main door. The main prayer hall typically has a half-hipped, half-gabled roof, and is invariably decorated with sculptures of dragons and other auspicious symbols. A Buddhist temple will always have representations of Buddha and his disciples — the Po Lin Monastery on Lantau Island being an exceptionally good example of this, with its enormous Tian Tan Buddha Statue — and often of Guan Yin, the Goddess of Mercy. Chinese temples may be classified according to function: *ci* for ancestor worship, *si* for Buddhists and *guan* for Taoists; *miao* are small temples usually reserved for the worship of Confucius; while *an* are for nuns. Very often these temples serve as community centres and house the old and the poor. The Pao Kong Temple in Macau is a small, traditional Chinese place of worship.

Indian Temple

Hong Kong has a number of Hindu and Sikh temples. Hindu worship takes place in elaborately decorated and colourful temples. Always square in plan, these temples are designed according to complex rules that govern everything from picking the right site to the architecture of the temple itself.

Jamia Mosque, Mosque Street

Each temple is dedicated to a particular god and forms a focal point for the Hindu community. Sikh temples tend to be more austere, less colourful, and are often quite elegant. The Sikh Temple beside the Happy Valley Racecourse is an excellent example of the traditional style.

Mosque

There are a number of mosques dotted throughout Hong Kong. Most of the Territory's Muslims originally came from British India, lured by the trade in the region. Their mosques are traditional in form and layout, are often capped with a dome, and have at least one minaret from which the *muezzin* calls the faithful to prayer (or, as is mostly the case nowadays, from which recordings of the *adhan* are broadcast). When entering a mosque, remember that you must be dressed appropriately—no shorts or short-sleeved shirts—and shoes must be left outside. The Jamia Mosque at the top of the Escalator in Central is a pretty example of a Muslim place of worship.

Shophouse

Shophouses are a unique Asian construction that started to make an appearance during colonial times. A shophouse is, as its name might suggest, a shop with a house over it. Usually two- to four-storeys high, they can still be seen throughout the cities of East and Southeast Asia. In Hong Kong they have all but disappeared, but there is still an enclave of them around the Johnston Road area of Wan Chai, which includes The Pawn bar and restaurant, as well as a few still nestling on Queen's Road Central, near Aberdeen Street. Hong Kong's shophouses tended to be taller than those in the other cities of the region — a testament to Hong Kong's perennially high land prices. The Neoclassical style predominates in the few that are still around.

Shophouse, Queen's Road Central

Gothic style: Roman Catholic Cathedral, Glenealy

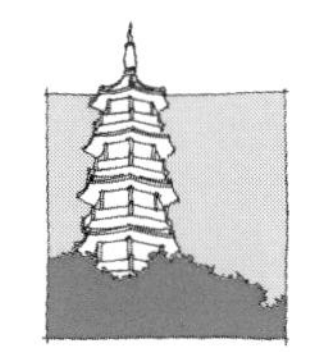

Gothic

Originating in northern France, Gothic architecture rapidly spread to England thanks to the Norman invasion, and was characterised by the use of soaring architectural features such as thin-ribbed ceilings, pointed arches, spires and delicate tracery. Its greatest glories are the medieval churches of northern Europe. With the revival of Classicism during the Renaissance, the Gothic style fell out of fashion, until it was revived in the 19th century, particularly in England. A long battle raged between Gothic Revival and Neoclassicism until new movements in architecture swept them both away at the beginning of the 20th century. The Roman Catholic Cathedral on Glenealy is a good example of the Gothic style.

Neoclassical

Classical architecture flowered in Ancient Greece and Rome in the centuries before and after the birth of Christ. It disappeared with the fall of the Roman Empire only to be reinvented in the 16th century, first in Italy by Andrea Palladio, and then throughout the rest of Europe and the world thanks to architects such as Inigo Jones. Neoclassicism is governed by strict proportioning systems, making use of the five classical orders: Doric, Ionic, Corinthian, Tuscan and Composite. St Margaret's Church (near the Happy Valley Racecourse), an elegant example of a Neoclassical building, makes use of the Doric order.

Neoclassical style: St Margaret's Church, Wong Nai Chung Road

Glossary

arcade	A series of arches and columns or pillars, often open on one side.
Art Deco	Style in art and architecture popular in the 1920s and 1930s that drew inspiration from industrial elements.
Baroque	Style in art and architecture that developed in the 17th century characterised by ornamentation on a grand scale.
colonnade	Row of columns (similar to an arcade).
column	A vertical supporting element.
Edwardian	Built during the reign of Edward VII (1901–1910); well-proportioned Neoclassicism, often mixing brick and plasterwork on facades.
feng shui	A Chinese system of geomancy aimed at maintaining harmony between man and nature through the siting, orientation and design of buildings.
gable	Triangular upper part of a wall at the end of a roof.
Gothic	Style of architecture prevalent in Western Europe from the 12th to the 16th century and again in the 19th century; its main features are pointed arches, delicate stonework and plenty of ornamentation.
Greek Revival	A type of Neoclassicism based on the architecture of Ancient Greece rather than Rome.
loggia	Open-sided arcade, often on an upper floor.
minaret	Tower attached to a mosque, from which the *muezzin* calls the faithful to prayer.
Neoclassical	Style of architecture popular from the 17th century onwards and based on the architecture of Ancient Greece and the Roman Empire; buildings are usually symmetrical, elegantly proportioned, and characterised by the generous use of columns and pillars.
Parsee	Old-fashioned term for a person from the Middle East — usually Zoroastrian — primarily from around modern-day Iran.
portico	Roof supported by columns, usually forming an entrance.

Romanesque Architectural style popular in Western Europe after the fall of the Roman Empire and before the Gothic movement; its main features are thick walls, round arches and decorative carved stonework.

triad Chinese secret society, originally formed to overthrow the Qing dynasty, now better known for being organised crime syndicates.

typhoon Violent tropical storm; Hong Kong's typhoon season runs from May through September.

veranda Roofed gallery, open at the sides and attached to the exterior of a building.

Victorian Built during the reign of Queen Victoria (1837–1901); invariably elaborate and over-decorated.

Listings

Hong Kong

Hong Kong Tourism Board
www.discoverhongkong.com

MTR (Mass Transit Railway)
Operation hours: 6am–midnight
Tel: 2881 8888
www.mtr.com.hk

Telephone directory enquiries
Tel: 1081

Hong Kong–Macau Ferry

Hong Kong–Macau Ferry Terminal, Shun Tak Centre (Hong Kong Island)
Nearest MTR: Sheung Wan
Operation hours: 6.30am–midnight, and limited services after midnight

China Ferry Terminal, China Hong Kong City (Kowloon)
Nearest MTR: Tsim Sha Tsui
Operation hours: 7am–10.30pm

Macau

Macau Government Tourist Information Counter (Hong Kong)
336 Shun Tak Centre, 200 Connaught Road
Tel: 2857 2287

Macau Government Tourist Information Counter (Hong Kong Airport)
Counter 3B, Meeters and Greeters Hall, Passenger Terminal Building
Tel: 2769 7970

Macau Government Tourist Office (Macau)
9 Largo do Senado
Tel: (853) 315 566, 513 355
www.macautourism.gov.mo

Macau Tourist Assistance Unit
Tel: (853) 340 390

Index

Page numbers in bold indicate illustrations

Notes